ROBERTO BOLAÑO: THE LAST INTERVIEW

& OTHER CONVERSATIONS

ROBERTO BOLAÑO: THE LAST INTERVIEW

& OTHER CONVERSATIONS

LAST INTERVIEW BY MÓNICA MARISTAIN
TRANSLATED BY SYBIL PEREZ

WITH AN INTRODUCTION BY MARCELA VALDES

ANNOTATIONS BY TOM McCARTAN

 MELVILLE HOUSE PUBLISHING
BROOKLYN, NEW YORK

Compilation and translation © Melville House Publishing, 2009

First Melville House Printing: November 2009

Melville House Publishing
145 Plymouth Street
Brooklyn, NY 11201

www.mhpbooks.com

ISBN: 978-1-933633-83-1

Book design by Kelly Blair

Cover photo by Basso Cannarsa

Library of Congress Control Number: 2009939057

Printed in the United States of America

CONTENTS

INTRODUCTION

ALONE AMONG THE GHOSTS
MARCELA VALDES

THE PART ABOUT THE AUTHOR

Shortly before he died of liver failure in July 2003, Roberto Bolaño remarked that he would have preferred to be a detective rather than a writer. Bolaño was fifty years old at the time, and by then he was widely considered to be the most important Latin American novelist since Gabriel García Márquez. But when Mónica Maristain interviewed him for the Mexican edition of *Playboy*, Bolaño was unequivocal. "I would have liked to be a homicide detective, much more than a writer," he told the magazine. "Of that I'm absolutely sure. A string of homicides. Someone who could go back alone, at night, to the scene of the crime, and not be afraid of ghosts."

Detective stories, and provocative remarks, were always passions of Bolaño's—he once declared James Ellroy among the best living writers in English—but his interest in gumshoe tales went beyond matters of plot and style. In their essence, detective stories are investigations into the motives and mechanics of violence, and Bolaño—who moved to Mexico the year of the 1968 Tlatelolco massacre and said he was briefly imprisoned during the 1973 military coup in his native Chile—was also obsessed with such matters. The great subject of his oeuvre is the relationship between art and infamy, craft and crime, the writer and the totalitarian state.

In fact, all of Bolaño's mature novels scrutinize how writers react to repressive regimes. *Distant Star* (1996) grapples with Chile's history of death squads and desaparecidos by conjuring up a poet turned serial killer. *The Savage Detectives* (1998) exalts a gang of young poets who joust against state-funded writers during the years of Mexico's dirty wars. *Amulet* (1999) revolves around a middle-aged poet who survives the government's 1968 invasion of the Autonomous University of Mexico by hiding in a bathroom. *By Night in Chile* (2000) depicts a literary salon where writers party in the same house in which dissidents are tortured. And Bolaño's final, posthumous novel, *2666*, is also spun from ghastly news: the murder, since 1993, of more than 430 women and girls in the Mexican state of Chihuahua, particularly in Ciudad Juárez.

Often these victims disappear while on their way to school or returning home from work or while they're out dancing with friends. Days or months later, their bodies turn up—tossed in a ditch, the middle of the desert or a city dump. Most are strangled; some are knifed or burned or shot. One-third show signs of rape. Some show signs of torture. The oldest known victims are in their thirties; the youngest are elementary-school age. Since 2002 these murders have been the subject of a Hollywood film (*Bordertown*, starring Jennifer Lopez), several nonfiction books, a number of documentaries and a flood of demonstrations in Mexico and abroad. According to Amnesty International, over half of the so-called "femicides" have not resulted in a conviction.

Bolaño was fascinated by these cold cases long before the murders became a cause célèbre. In 1995 he sent a letter from Spain to his old friend in Mexico City, the visual artist Carla Rippey (who is portrayed as the beautiful Catalina O'Hara in *The Savage Detectives*), mentioning that for years he'd been working on a novel called "The Woes of the True Policeman." Though he had other manuscripts on submission to publishers, this book, Bolaño wrote, "is MY NOVEL." Set in northern Mexico, in a town called Santa Teresa, it revolved around a literature professor who had a fourteen-year-old daughter. The manuscript had already topped "eight hundred thousand pages," he boasted; it was "a demented tangle that surely no one will understand."

Surely, it seemed so then. Bolaño was forty-three when he sent this missive, and as near to failure as he'd ever been. Though he'd published two books of poetry, co-written a novel and spent five years entering short story contests all over Spain, he was so broke that he couldn't afford a telephone line, and his work was almost entirely unknown. Three years earlier, he and his wife had separated; around the same time he was diagnosed with the liver disease that would kill him eight years later. Though Bolaño won many of the short story contests he entered, his novels were routinely rejected by publishers. Yet late in 1995 he would begin an astonishing rise.

The turning point was a meeting with Jorge Herralde, the founder and director of the publishing house Editorial Anagrama. Though Herralde couldn't buy *Nazi Literature in the Americas*—it was snapped up by Seix Barral—he invited Bolaño to visit him in Barcelona. There Bolaño told him about his cash problems and the desperation he felt over the many rejections he'd received. "I told him that...I'd love to read his other manuscripts, and shortly afterward he brought me *Distant Star* (later I found out that it had also been rejected by other publishing houses, including Seix Barral)," the editor recalls in an essay. Herralde, however, found the book extraordinary. Thereafter, he published all of Bolaño's fiction: nine books in seven years.

During that time, as each volume found more readers than its predecessor, Bolaño toiled away on his demented tangle. The work involved writing, of course, but also investigating. By setting his novel in Santa Teresa, a fictional town in Sonora, rather than in Juárez, Bolaño was able to blur the lines between what he knew and what he imagined. But he was deeply concerned with understanding the circumstances facing Juárez and its inhabitants. Bolaño was already familiar with the region's bleak, arid landscape—he'd traveled to northern Mexico during the 1970s—but the femicides didn't begin until sixteen years after he had left for Europe, and he'd never visited Juárez. Since he didn't know anyone living in the city, his knowledge was limited to what he could find in newspapers and on the Internet. From these sources he would have learned that Juárez had become the perfect place to commit a crime.

Once a watering hole for Americans during Prohibition, Juárez grew rapidly after NAFTA was implemented in the 1990s. Hundreds of assembly plants sprang up, luring hundreds of thousands of destitute residents from all over Mexico to take jobs that often paid as little as 50 cents an hour. The same traits that made Juárez appealing to NAFTA manufacturers—good roads, proximity to a large consumer market, an abundance of unorganized labor—also made it an ideal hub for narcotraficantes. By 1996, some forty-two million people and seventeen million vehicles were traveling through the city every year, making it one of the busiest transit points on the US-Mexico border and a favorite for illegal crossings. The town transformed itself into a crossroads for cheap and illicit commerce; as it did, poor, hardworking women began turning up dead.

Juárez and its fictional counterpart bear little resemblance to the cultural centers where Bolaño set most of his novels—even *Distant Star* takes place in the most important university town in southern Chile. There are no writing workshops amid the shantytowns of Santa Teresa, nor gangs of rebellious poets. Like all of Bolaño's fiction, *2666* teems with writers, artists and intellectuals, but these characters come from elsewhere: from Europe, South America, the United States and Mexico City. Stuck in the badlands of northern Mexico, the same region where Cormac McCarthy's gang of merry killers rampage in *Blood Meridian*, Santa Teresa is literally and culturally parched.

The link between this industrial desert and the settings of Bolaño's previous novels lies, like a scarlet letter, on the book's front cover. The devilish date 2666—which appears nowhere in the pages of *2666*—sends us on a scavenger hunt to *Amulet*, where it crops up in the waking nightmares of a woman named Auxilio Lacouture. Visions of hell besiege Auxilio from the novel's earliest pages, when she peers into a flower vase and sees "everything that people have lost, everything that causes pain and that is better off forgotten."

Later, as she walks through the streets of Mexico City, she has another evil hallucination. It's the middle of the night. The streets she crosses are vacant and windy. At that hour, Auxilio says, Avenida Reforma "turns into a transparent tube, a cuneiform lung where you feel the city's imaginary breath," and Avenida Guerrero "looks like nothing more than a cemetery...a cemetery from the year 2666, a cemetery forgotten under a dead or unborn cyelid, bathed in the dispassionate fluids of an eye that, for wanting to forget something, has ended forgetting everything."

2666, like all of Bolaño's work, is a graveyard. In his 1998 acceptance speech for the Rómulo Gallego's Prize, Bolaño revealed that in some way everything he wrote was "a letter of love or of goodbye" to the young people who died in the dirty wars of Latin America. His previous novels memorialized the dead of the 1960s and '70s. His ambitions for *2666* were greater: to write a postmortem for the dead of the past, the present and the future.

THE PART ABOUT THE CRIMES

Bolaño put off the possibility of a liver transplant so he could complete *2666*, but the illness grew more acute and he died before he reached the book's end. After the funeral, his friend and literary executor, the Spanish book critic Ignacio Echevarría, combed through the manuscripts in Bolaño's office to assemble the work that Anagrama published in 2004, and that Natasha Wimmer, the gifted translator of *The Savage Detectives*, has brought into English.

Bolaño marked his manuscripts carefully. He may have been reckless, but he wasn't stupid, and he knew that he was dying. Yet Anagrama broke with his wishes on one point. For years Bolaño had talked about *2666* as one book, bragging that it would be "the fattest novel in the world," but in the final months of his life, he decided to break up the novel's five sections and publish them as separate books. The reasons behind this impulse were practical. Bolaño would leave behind two young children, to whom he dedicated *2666*, and he wanted to provide for them after his death. Five short novels, he figured, would earn more money than one backbreaking monster. Thankfully, his family and Anagrama did him the favor of following his original vision. As Echevarría notes in his epilogue, "although the five parts that comprise *2666* may be read independently, they not only share many elements (a subtle web of recurring themes), they also join unequivocally in a unified design." Meanwhile, in the United States, the book's publisher, Farrar, Straus and Giroux, hedged its bets: putting out both a 2.75-pound hardcover and a three-volume slipcased paperback edition.

Either way, *2666* isn't for the faint of heart. The book is nearly 900 pages long, and charting its locations would yield something like an airline flight map, red dots marking landings in Argentina, England, France, Germany, Italy, Mexico, Poland, Prussia, Romania, Russia, Spain and the United States. As if such globe-trotting wasn't enough, the novel also contains scores of characters and covers almost an entire century of history.

Bolaño once wrote that in the Americas, all modern fiction springs from two sources: *The Adventures of Huckleberry Finn* and *Moby-Dick*. *The Savage Detectives*, with its carousing characters, is Bolaño's novel of friendship and adventure. *2666* chases the white whale. For Bolaño, Melville's novel held the key to writing about "the land of evil"; and like Melville's saga, *2666* can be stunning or soporific, depending on your taste for the slow burn. I've read it three times, and I find it to be dense, brilliant and horrifying, with scattered scenes of cleverness and fun.

Page one plunges us into the lives of four European academics who adore the books of a reclusive German author named Benno von Archimboldi almost as much as they enjoy luring each other to bed. Bolaño's approach to the murders in the first two parts of *2666*—"The Part About the Critics" and "The Part About Amalfitano"—is coy, elliptical. Not for him the rapid gore of Patricia Cornwell or Stephen King. The first, glancing mention of the crimes doesn't occur until forty-three pages into the book, and only two of the three professors who visit Santa Teresa in the first part even hear about the murders. They are visitors to Mexico, and though they dabble in sex tourism, their wealth and indifference insulate them from the realities of the city.

"The Part About Amalfitano"—which clearly derives from the book Bolaño described to Rippey in 1995—moves closer to the locals, while still keeping the murders at arm's length. If part one is a brainy romance, part two is an existential drama. A Chilean philosophy professor who has left Europe for the University of Santa Teresa founders in quiet desperation. He fears that he's going crazy—a voice speaks to him at night. He fears that the city's violence may reach out and grab his daughter—a black car keeps appearing just outside his house.

Careful readers will spy hints of what's to come, like so many red fingerprints, throughout these two sections, but it isn't until the third part, "The Part About Fate," that the violence of Santa Teresa spills into the foreground. Standing in a bar, a naïve American reporter sees a man across the room punch a woman: "The first blow made the woman's head snap violently and the second blow knocked her down." The reporter had driven to Mexico to see another kind of beating—a fight between an American boxer and his Mexican rival—but he soon learns that the real blows in Santa Teresa occur outside the ring. Befriended by some of the seedier elements of the city, he is shown what appears to be the video of a woman being raped. He meets the chief suspect in the city's murders, and he winds up peeling out of town afraid of the police.

This noir escapade is prelude to a dirge. "The Part About the Crimes" opens in January 1993 with the description of the corpse of a thirteen-year-old girl and ends 108 bodies later during Christmas 1997. Each one of these forensic discoveries is clinically detailed—at 284 pages, the section is the longest in the book—and the resulting chronicle of death is braided through with the narratives of four detectives, one reporter, the chief suspect in the crimes and various ancillary characters. In Bolaño's hands, this collage produces terrific fugue-like sequences and damning repetitions. ("The case was soon closed" becomes a haunting refrain.)

Bolaño lightens these grim story lines with flashes of gallows humor and the occasional tender subplot. Overall, however, reading "The Part About the Crimes" feels like staring into the abyss. Strangling, shooting, stabbing, burning, rape, whipping, mutilation, bribery and treachery are all detailed in deadpan prose. "In the middle of November," a typical paragraph runs:

> Andrea Pacheco Martínez, thirteen, was kidnapped on her way out of Vocational School 16.... When she was found, two days later, her body showed unmistakable signs of strangulation, with a fracture of the hyoid bone. She had been anally and vaginally raped. There was tumefaction of the wrists, as if they had been bound. Both ankles presented lacerations, by which it was deduced that her feet had also been tied. A Salvadorean immigrant found the body behind the Francisco I School, on Madero, near Colonia Álamos. It was fully dressed, and the clothes, except for the shirt, which was missing several buttons, were intact.

Those who've sampled Bolaño's other fictions will recognize the cool detachment of this passage. But the level of grisly detail is like nothing in any of Bolaño's previous works—or in any of the newspaper accounts he could have read. His descriptions of the murder investigations, and of the incidents surrounding the trial of the chief suspect, are equally precise and uncanny.

How did Bolaño become so intimate with the details of these crimes, and the procedures of the local police, when he lived an ocean away? His other investigative novels were written after the fresh blood of history had dried; even then, Bolaño had always drawn from firsthand knowledge of the events or from that of his friends. Yet at the time he was writing "The Part About the Crimes," information about the murders in Juárez was quite restricted. To pull off this kind of hyperrealism, he must have had the help of someone on the inside, someone whose interest in autopsy was as relentless as his own.

THE PART ABOUT THE JOURNALIST

In the summer of 1995, the year Bolaño wrote to Carla Rippey, the bodies of several young women were discovered semi-nude and strangled just south of Juárez, near the local airport. That September the city offered a $1,000 reward for information about The Predator. A month later, police arrested Abdel Latif Sharif Sharif, an Arab-American with a history of sexual aggression, and charged him with the five murders, plus a few others committed in September. But two months later, while Sharif Sharif awaited trial in prison, fresh corpses began to appear. The police maintained that Sharif Sharif, a chemist, had directed these murders from his cell, paying $1,200 for each woman killed. His accomplices, they said, were eight teenage boys they arrested in a sweep of nightclubs. They were called The Rebels.

Almost 1,000 miles away, in Mexico City, this news fascinated a reporter named Sergio González Rodríguez. A novelist and arts journalist, González Rodríguez had launched his career during the 1980s by doing reviews for Carlos Monsiváis, a leading cultural critic and a pioneer of the nueva crónica, or New Journalism, style in Mexico. By the time the newspaper *Reforma* came calling in 1993, González Rodríguez was well known as a centrist critic who wasn't afraid of riling the government: he'd been fired from the magazine *Nexos* for publishing an article in *Reforma* that questioned the ethics of intellectuals who allied themselves with then-President Carlos Salinas de Gortari, who'd been elected in 1988 amid widespread allegations of voter fraud. This independent temperament made González Rodríguez a good match for *Reforma*— the paper had a history of serious investigative reporting—and he was hired to edit one of the paper's weekend cultural supplements, "El Ángel." (These days González Rodríguez still serves as the section's editorial consultant. He also writes three regular columns for the paper.)

The news from Juárez reminded González Rodríguez of the movie *Silence of the Lambs*, which he'd seen a few years earlier. Could it be, he wondered, that Ciudad Juárez held a real Hannibal Lecter? Answering that question wasn't part of his regular beat, but as he explained to me in a series of interviews, he'd always been interested in literature about violence. His favorite books include Truman Capote's *In Cold Blood*, Norman Mailer's *The Executioner's Song* and Hans Magnus Enzensberger's *Politics and Crime*. He already had plans to travel to the state of Chihuahua to teach a seminar. It wasn't hard to persuade *Reforma* to pay for a jumper flight from there to Juárez so he could report on a press conference that the chief suspect planned to hold, in prison, on April 19, 1996.

That day González Rodríguez watched a tall, middle-aged man with green eyes talk to some thirty reporters. Sharif Sharif barely spoke Spanish— he'd lived in Mexico for less than a year—so he gave his presentation in English while a bilingual reporter translated. What he said sounded like a soap opera. According to Sharif Sharif, the femicides were being committed by a pair of rich Mexican cousins, one who lived in Juárez and the other just over the border in El Paso. He told a love story involving one of the cousins and a poor, beautiful girl from Juárez. The press corps was annoyed—they exchanged glances, cracked jokes. González Rodríguez felt pretty skeptical himself, but the critic in him was intrigued by Sharif Sharif's style. Rather than pound his chest and declare his innocence, the suspect calmly recounted his ninety-minute tale. He seemed to believe that if he provided an alternate explanation for the murders, the charges against him would be dropped.

At the end of the session, González Rodríguez introduced himself to a local reporter. In a park near the prison, the two chatted about the strange presentation. A mother and her daughter approached them.

Are you journalists? the mother asked.

Yes, they answered.

Then we want to tell you something we think that you should know.

The fourteen-year-old girl beside her wore a T-shirt, jeans and sneakers. She told the reporters that the Juárez chief of police had forced her to accuse The Rebels. The chief, she said, had taken her by the hair and banged her against a wall until she agreed to say exactly what he told her.

For González Rodríguez, perspective suddenly shifted. Old facts (the nightclub sweep, the escalating charges against Sharif Sharif) glittered in a new light: the police were beating witnesses.

"This," he thought, "is the undercurrent." Later, he learned that while Sharif Sharif had been holding forth in prison, the State Commission on Human Rights had announced that six of the eight witnesses against The Rebels had been detained illegally by the Juárez police.

González Rodríguez flew back to Mexico City and published an article about his findings and the suspicious treatment of the witnesses. Soon after, *Reforma* asked him to join a special investigations unit devoted to the situation in Juárez. The head of the unit, Rossana Fuentes Berain, sent a journalist undercover into the factories where many of the murder victims had worked; she assigned other reporters to track the details of individual police investigations. González Rodríguez was given the task of studying the big picture for patterns and motivations. Though Berain edited González Rodríguez like any other reporter—sometimes demanding that he corroborate sources or provide additional proofs for his more damning assessments—she also allowed him considerable interpretive leeway.

For three years he traveled back and forth between Juárez and Mexico City, juggling book and film reviews with criminal investigation, until, in the summer of 1999, his reporting began to suggest that the policemen, government officials and drug traffickers of Juárez were all connected to one another, and to the femicides. An attack on the son of Sharif Sharif's lawyer earlier that year had hardened his suspicions. Why would someone attack a lawyer's son if the justice system was functioning properly? he wondered. Then, on June 12, together with a reporter from the *El Paso Times*, González Rodríguez interviewed a prisoner who implicated local police and a prominent senator in the femicides.

In his book *Huesos en el desierto*, González Rodríguez recounts that three days later he was kidnapped and assaulted by two men in Mexico City. He had hailed a taxi in the posh neighborhood of Condesa, heading home after a late night. The taxi drove for a while and then stopped. Two armed men jumped aboard. They ordered González Rodríguez to close his eyes and sit between them in the back seat. The taxi took off—the driver was complicit. Though González Rodríguez didn't resist his captors, the men cursed him, punched him, pistol-whipped him and pierced his legs with an ice pick. They would kill him in a deserted spot south of the capital, they said. The taxi stopped again. One of the men got out, and another, whom they called The Boss, sat down. The beatings and threats of rape and death resumed. A patrol car passed nearby with its flashers on. The men dumped González Rodríguez on the street. He filed a police report and went to see a doctor, who prescribed painkillers and bed rest. On June 18, his article "Police Are Fingered as Accomplices [in Juárez]" appeared in *Reforma*.

For the next two months, González Rodríguez lived like a zombie, writing reviews, editing his section and going out with friends even as his vision clouded, his speech slurred and his memory disintegrated. Finally, on August 11, when he couldn't even brew a cup of coffee in his own home, two friends from *Reforma* rushed him to a hospital, where he had emergency surgery to remove a life-threatening hematoma that was pressing on his brain.

Against all expectations, he made a complete recovery, but the beating marked a turning point in his life. Before the attack, González Rodríguez had had problems with his home and cellphones— strange noises, deficiencies in service. After, he was often followed. His friend Paola Tinoco recalls that whenever she and González Rodríguez ate in a restaurant in the months following his surgery, they were watched by people wearing earphones. Terrified and helpless, the two took refuge in humor, telling each other absurd stories every time the strangers were present. One night, for example, they recited the lyrics to a popular children's song called "The Ducky":

> Ducky goes running and searching in her
>   purse-y
> For pennies to feed her own little duckies
> Because she knows that when she gets back
> All the ducks will run up and ask

What did you bring me, Mamá, quack quack?
What did you bring me, quack quack?

When González Rodríguez flew to Juárez in 1995 looking for a Hollywood-style serial killer, he recalls, "I had no idea what I was getting into." Instead of Hannibal Lecter, he found a system of impunity that protected the worst criminals in Juárez, simply because they were ruthless and rich, a system that implicated the police and judicial institutions of the city, the state and the country. Once he drew these conclusions, there was no going back. "You're in a hell," he says, "that you don't know why you've been chosen to live." The heat incinerated many of his old illusions about accountability and justice, revealing Mexico's black heart.

The authorities, he believed, were deliberately trying to confuse and obscure the realities in Juárez, suggesting that the numbers were exaggerated, or that the murders were crimes of passion, or that the victims were prostitutes. He wanted to make a permanent record of his findings to contradict those stories, a record that wouldn't be tossed out at week's end.

THE PART ABOUT THE CORRESPONDENCE

The year that González Rodríguez was first attacked, Bolaño had been working on his demented tangle for more than half a decade. Searching for information about Juárez, Bolaño e-mailed his friends in Mexico, asking more and more detailed questions about the murders. Finally, tired of these gruesome inquiries, his friends put him in touch with González Rodríguez, who, they said, knew more about the crimes than anyone in Mexico. Bolaño first e-mailed him around the time that González Rodríguez decided to write a nonfiction book about his investigation.

In retrospect, it's strange the two didn't correspond earlier. They were roughly the same age: González Rodríguez was born in 1950, Bolaño in 1953. Both had been part of Mexico City's counterculture in the 1970s: Bolaño tramping about town with the Infrarealist poets, González Rodríguez playing bass for a heavy-metal band called Grupo Enigma. Both began writing novels late and prided themselves on the integrity of their literary judgments. They had several friends in common: Jorge Herralde and the critic and novelist Juan Villoro. And in middle age both were consumed by Juárez.

González Rodríguez could tell right away that Bolaño's interest in the crimes wasn't a whim. "It wasn't a temp job, like that of so many novelists," González Rodríguez says. "It was the passion of a lifetime. He would say to me, What you do think of such and such text? He had read everything."

What Bolaño needed, González Rodríguez explains, was help with the details of the murders and the police investigations, because the press accounts of them were too vague. He wanted to know how the narcos in Juárez operated, what cars they drove, what weapons they carried. "What he liked was precision," González Rodríguez says. In the case of weapons, for example, Bolaño wanted to know not just the brand but also the model and the caliber.

He was also interested in connecting with the mentality of Chihuahua's police to understand the particularities of their conduct and misconduct. He wanted to know exactly how murder cases were written up. He wanted a copy of a forensic report; González Rodríguez unearthed one in the papers he'd gotten from a defense lawyer. At Bolaño's request, he transcribed a section describing the victim's injuries. "He wanted to know the language of forensic investigation," González Rodríguez recalls. It is this language that appears in "The Part About the Crimes."

"I imagine, based on what he would ask me, that what he wanted was to compare notes," González Rodríguez says. "I'd say that the savage detective wanted the other savage detective, who is me, to draw analogous conclusions." Yet any writer knows that sharing conclusions often changes them. Comparing notes with González Rodríguez, Bolaño may have altered a few long-held beliefs. Take, for example, the two detectives' discussion of Robert K.

Ressler, the former FBI criminologist who visited Juárez in 1998 to consult on the murders, thanks to a deal made between Mexico's Congress and its attorney general. Bolaño had already read Ressler's famous books—among them, *Sexual Homicide* and *Crime Classification Manual*—and he was amazed that Ressler didn't solve the murders during his trip.

Why didn't Ressler catch the killer? he asked.

That trip was just window dressing, González Rodríguez remembers telling him. He explained that Ressler had come to Juárez unprepared. He didn't bring his own translator. He was paid by the same authorities who might be implicated by his findings. He had to review criminal files in Spanish, a language he didn't know. He was given a bodyguard who watched everything he did. This information, González Rodríguez remembers, hit Bolaño like cold water.

"He wanted to believe that there was a rational power that could conquer the criminal," he observes. In fact, such a triumphant ratiocinator appears in all Bolaño's novels—except for *2666*. In *Distant Star*, the serial killer is caught by detective Abel Romero, with the help of a smart poet. In *By Night in Chile*, the crimes of the literati are unearthed by an anonymous young detective. Another anonymous interrogator traces the history of Arturo Belano and Ulises Lima in *The Savage Detectives*, while these two young poets successfully locate the mysterious writer Cesárea Tinajero—whom they find in a town near Santa Teresa.

Only in *2666* do criminals slip the noose, trapping and killing or beating every Nosy Parker who comes their way. Significantly, in the final version of *2666*, the character based on Ressler (Albert Kessler) first appears as a cunning, if tactless, detective, only to have the rug pulled out from under his investigation several pages later.

More fundamentally, González Rodríguez told Bolaño how his findings suggested that the killings in Juárez were connected to the local police and politicians and to the mercenary gangs maintained by the drug cartels. The police don't seriously investigate the murders, he explained, because they're badly trained, or they're misogynists, or they've made deals that allow the narcos to operate with impunity.

So there's no serial killer? González Rodríguez recalls Bolaño asked him.

No, of course there's a serial killer, González Rodríguez replied. But it's not just one serial killer. I think there are at least two serial killers.

This revelation, González Rodríguez says, disconcerted Bolaño. By then, the writer had already devised an elaborate, ingenious structure for his novel, a structure that in some ways depends on the idea of a single serial killer. The innocence or guilt of the real Sharif Sharif wasn't the issue, González Rodríguez says. The problem was how to fit fresh news about the crimes into *2666*.

Bolaño's solution, I suspect, was to adopt many of González Rodríguez's conclusions about Juárez wholesale, then to dramatize these theories in his own way. The parallels between the stories in "The Part About the Crimes" and the conclusions in González Rodríguez's book *Huesos en el desierto*—which isn't available in English—are startling. Yet "nothing," González Rodríguez points out, "is ever followed to the letter." Names are changed, nationalities transformed, characters invented, entire plots embroidered out of imagination, style and air. Bolaño may have used everything González Rodríguez taught him—he read the manuscript for *Huesos* months before it was published—but he refashioned it all to suit his own ends.

THE PART ABOUT THE GOAT

After years of correspondence, the two savage detectives finally met in November 2002, when González Rodríguez traveled to Barcelona for the official launch of *Huesos*. Anagrama had bought the book for its prestigious Crónicas imprint, setting it alongside works by Günter Wallraff, Ryszard Kapuscinski and Michael Herr. More than 100 people attended the debut presentation. Months later, the Mexican consulate would decline to send a representative to a theatrical performance inspired by *Huesos*, stating that its officials "don't support works that denigrate Mexico."

Huesos was launched in Spain partly to protect its author. When it was printed, many of the government and police officials fingered by González Rodríguez were still in power, and its account of systematic corruption in Juárez angered those who wanted to portray Mexico as a civilized nation. But press coverage for the book in Europe provided González Rodríguez with a measure of protection against reprisals. After such coverage, there would be no way of making the book or its author quietly disappear when *Huesos* was later released in Mexico.

Bolaño didn't attend the launch, but early the next day González Rodríguez and a friend headed north to the seaside town of Blanes to meet him and his family for lunch. They arrived several hours late. Hung over from the previous night's celebration of dinner and absinthe, González Rodríguez and his friend had boarded the wrong train. Bolaño forgave their late appearance, opening a bottle of wine and offering ham sandwiches. Knowing that Bolaño's illness made it impossible for him to drink liquor, González Rodríguez had brought him a half-kilo of coffee from La Habana, the cafe in Mexico City that Bolaño immortalized in *The Savage Detectives*. Bolaño's liver was so bad that he couldn't drink coffee either, but González Rodríguez recalls that he opened the bag and buried his nose in it.

For the next several hours, they talked about the murders in Juárez. For once, they had no worries about tapped phones or intercepted e-mails. Bolaño could ask all the questions he wanted.

Listen, Bolaño joked, I'm going to make you a character in my novel. I'm going to plagiarize the idea from Javier Marías, who made you a character in *La negra espalda del tiempo*.

González Rodríguez felt his stomach sink. Really, Roberto? he said. With my name?

Yes, don't worry about it, Bolaño said. His daughter, Alejandra, was playing with González Rodríguez's friend. Bolaño looked happy. González Rodríguez didn't know what to say.

The next evening they met for sushi in Barcelona. This time they talked, not about Juárez but about literature. Bolaño asked if writers in Mexico still wore beards or if they'd all cut them off. At one point, he announced that he and Mario Santiago had officially dissolved the Infrarealist movement in Paris in 1992. He's crazy, González Rodríguez thought. He thinks that the only Infrarealists who matter are him and Santiago.

Shortly after this visit, Bolaño published the essay "Sergio González Rodríguez Under the Hurricane," which declared his affection and admiration for the journalist and sang the praises of his book. González Rodríguez's "technical help in the writing of my novel," he wrote, "has been substantial." And *Huesos en el desierto* is "not only an imperfect photograph—how could it be anything else—of evil and of corruption; it also transforms itself into a metaphor of Mexico and of Mexico's past and of the uncertain future of all of Latin America."

Seven months later, on July 1, 2003, Bolaño was admitted to a hospital in Barcelona. Two weeks later, he died.

When *2666* was released in Mexico in 2004, González Rodríguez could barely bring himself to read it. "It took me months to read the section about the dead women," he says. "It terrified me. To live through it is one thing, but to see it told by a great literary master like Bolaño isn't funny. Roberto is crazier than a goat, you understand? You can't believe it because in some way you're there."

As a reporter, González Rodríguez had cultivated a critical distance that helped him ignore how easily he could be attacked again. Finding in *2666* a character with his name pinioned to a world of killers and cover-ups shattered that illusion. At one point Bolaño even describes a kidnapping exactly like the 1999 attack on González Rodríguez, except that it ends in death. It's not clear whether the reporter who dies is the character "Sergio González."

Such pointed mind games aside, any Mexican journalist writing about cartels or corruption would have felt vulnerable in 2004. That year, five investigative reporters were killed or disappeared in Mexico. One of them was shot to death in front of his two young children. According to a report put out by Reporters Without Borders in 2007, Mexico has become the second-most dangerous place in the world for journalists, the first being Iraq. Alejandro Junco de la Vega, the president of Grupo Reforma, told an audience at Columbia University in October 2008 that his three newspapers no longer run bylines, in order to protect their journalists. "We find ourselves under the siege of drug lords, criminals," he explained, "and the more we expose their activities, the harder they push back." Junco himself has moved his entire family to "a safe haven in the US."

So it may be a coincidence that the same year *2666* was published, González Rodríguez decided to stop traveling to Juárez. He'd heard there was a bounty on his head in the state of Chihuahua. Suits alleging slander had been filed, and he risked being jailed the moment he set foot in the state. Given these maneuvers, his lawyers recommended that he not enter Chihuahua under any circumstances. (It wasn't until April 2007 that President Felipe Calderón signed a federal law that decriminalized defamation and "insults," and obliged state governments to do the same.) The last time González Rodríguez visited, nobody wanted to talk about what was going on. It had become a city of closed doors.

Neither *Huesos* nor *2666* is an easy book to read. I was plagued by nightmares as I read both of them. Their pages are like freshly dug graves, but they are shadowed by different philosophies of evil. In Huesos, Juárez is a casualty of rampant corruption. When cops and courts look the other way, González Rodríguez believes, brutal acts become ordinary events. The rape and murder of women, the assassination of journalists, the kidnapping of people for ransom: none of these crimes are page-one news in Mexico anymore. "A malevolent person, like a serial killer, can unleash a kind of sweeping effect," González Rodríguez says, igniting a mechanism of extermination that rivals that of any totalitarian dictatorship. This "normalization of barbarism," he argues, is the most serious problem facing Mexico and Latin America today.

In the final section of *2666*, "The Part About Archimboldi," Bolaño presents a more sinister vision of evil. The section opens at the end of World War I, with a wounded Prussian's return home. Everything is changing, a stranger tells him: "The war was coming to an end and a new era was about to begin. [The Prussian] answered, as he ate, that nothing would ever change." Indeed, the whole finale of *2666*, which spans the First World War to the late 1990s, seems designed to prove Archimboldi's belief that history is nothing more than a series of instants "that vie with one another in monstrousness." As Archimboldi fights for the Third Reich on the Eastern Front and starts his career as a novelist in the ruins of Berlin, Bolaño regales us with tale after tale of rape and murder. In the hills of Germany, a man kills his wife and the authorities turn a blind eye. During the war, city folk who flee to the country are routinely robbed, raped and killed. The land around a Romanian castle is filled with buried human bones, and allusions to the Holocaust abound.

In this landscape of brutality and impunity, Santa Teresa seems less aberrant. It's just one of many places where an underlying, pervasive evil has welled up and broken the surface. As it is now in Santa Teresa, the novel seems to say, as it has always been, as it shall be in the cemeteries of 2666. Evil is as widespread and eternal as the sea.

This vision of violence brings to mind America's own apocalyptic writer, Cormac McCarthy, but Bolaño's novel has more sex and comedy, and his hero is quite different from those in *The Road* or *Blood Meridian*. Archimboldi marches through the battlefields of Poland and Romania like a man trolling along the bottom of the sea, immersed in the deep's dark horror yet untouched by it. As a teenager, he reads Wolfram von Eschenbach's *Parzival* and is captivated by the idea of a "lay and independent" medieval knight. His own holy grail turns out to be a dead man's diary he discovers in an abandoned shtetl.

A lay and independent knight: these words could describe both the great detectives and the great writers who wander through the pages of *2666*. All of them are loners who devote themselves to reading and swimming in the abyss. Being a writer in this world is as dangerous as being a detective, walking through a graveyard, looking at ghosts.

"LITERATURE IS NOT MADE FROM WORDS ALONE"

INTERVIEW BY HÉCTOR SOTO AND
MATÍAS BRAVO

FIRST PUBLISHED IN *CAPITAL*,
SANTIAGO, DECEMBER 1999

Ernesto Sabato

HÉCTOR SOTO AND MATÍAS BRAVO: What is your relationship with writers from the Latin American Boom?

ROBERTO BOLAÑO: Good, very good—as a reader, of course. Anyway the Boom is an imprecise notion. It depends on what parameters everybody gives. Does **Sábato** come in or not? How about **Onetti**? Most people would say no. **Rulfo**, who for me is one of the cornerstones of the Boom, is also left out.

HS/MB: Perhaps the emblematic figures of the movement were too adored, an injustice for quieter figures like **Monterroso** and Onetti, who are vindicated more and more. They've stayed relevant with the passage of time.

RB: I don't believe so. The literature of Vargas Llosa or García Márquez is gigantic.

HS/MB: A cathedral.

RB: More than a cathedral. I do not think time will harm them. The work of Vargas Llosa, for example, is immense. It has thousands of entry points and thousands of exit points. So does the literature of García Márquez. They're both public figures. They're not just literary figures. Vargas Llosa was a candidate for president. García Márquez is a po-

Argentine writer, Ernesto Sábato (b. 1911) was a driving force in the Argentine surrealist scene. Much of his work is available in English.

Uraguayan novelist and short story writer Juan Carlos Onetti (1909–1994) sought to blend the real and the fantastic in his fiction. His novella *The Pit* (1939) is one of the first works of modern Spanish-language literature.

After publishing the short story collection *The Burning Plain* (1953) and the novel *Pedro Páramo* (1955), Mexican author Juan Rulfo (1917–1986) stopped publishing narrative fiction, despite the enormous critical success of his books. Both Faulkner and García Márquez were influenced by Rulfo's prose.

Born in Honduras, raised in Guatemala, and eventually exiled to Mexico, Augusto Monterroso (1921–2003) was a deeply respected short story writer. His story "The Dinosaur" is said to be literature's shortest story. In full, it reads: "When he woke up, the dinosaur was still there." His *Complete Works and Other Stories* (1995) is available in English.

litical heavyweight and very influential in Latin America. This distorts things a bit, but it shouldn't make us lose sight of the position they have in the hierarchy. They are superiors, superior to the people who came after and, to be sure, to the writers of my generation. Books such as *No One Writes to the Colonel* are simply perfect.

No One Writes to the Colonel is a García Márquez novella.

HS/MB: Since you read the Boom during its own time, your reading must have been from the perspective of a poet. During that period, you were only writing poetry.

RB: Yes, but I read plenty of narrative work, although it's clear that my readings were from the perspective of a poet, which is a shame in a sense. If my reading had been from a narrator's perspective, I would have probably learned more. Perhaps I have gaps in the way I look at the internal structures of a novel. I would have learned this sooner had I read with a different perspective.

HS/MB: I have the impression that you compose small plots, which you then fit into the overall novel, although it isn't so clear whether you do it with a preconceived idea of what the work will eventually be.

RB: I always have an idea. Each time I begin to write a novel, I have a very elaborate structure in mind.

HS/MB: Very elaborate, yes. But it does not prevent each of your phrases, given the rhythm and inflection you infuse them with, from being justified, though not always in the service of the novel's unfolding plot.

RB: Well, I think that's something else. It relates to the elemental debt all prose writers have, which consists of cleaning a bit, trying to get close to language with open eyes and ears. I appreciate your words very much, but I don't assign great relevance to hygienic definitions of my work. I'm very demanding in that sense. Without going any further than *Savage Detectives*, there are phrases and whole paragraphs in it that seem to me to be very bad. They seem terrible to me.

HS/MB: Your books are distinct approximations of a particular world, a world of writers and rather marginal people who are in between being obsessives and losers. Your stories and novels also center around the same situations or the same characters.

RB: Also around the same arguments.

HS/MB: Exactly. Your characters are crusaders for revolutionizing art and changing the world, which is the project of your generation.

RB: Revolutionizing art and changing life were the objectives of Rimbaud's project. And reinventing love. At heart, to make life a work of art.

HS/MB: But you are a part of the world that you describe, and you look affectionately toward it.

RB: Perhaps I've been attempting to forgive myself.

HS/MB: You're not an apologist for the project or rhapsodic about it, but you're not a gravedigger, or a critic.

RB: I'm a survivor. I feel enormous affection toward this project, notwithstanding its excesses, immoderations and deviations. The project is hopelessly romantic, essentially revolutionary, and it has seen the failure of many groups and generations of artists. Though, even now, our conception of art in the West is indebted to this vision.

HS/MB: If there is a concept that has been devalued in this era, it is that of revolution.

RB: The truth for me—and I want to be very sincere—is that the idea of revolution had already been devalued by the time I was twenty years old. At that age, I was a Trotskyite and what I saw in the

Soviet Union was a counterrevolution. I never felt I had the support of the movement of history. To the contrary, I felt quite crushed. I think that's noticeable in the characters in *The Savage Detectives*.

HS/MB: At some point in your life, we imagined that you were animated by great revolutionary ardor.

RB: You imagined it correctly. I was against everything. Against New York and Moscow, against London and Havana, against Paris and Beijing. I even felt scared by the solitude entailed in radicalism.

HS/MB: Does your sense of having survived come from that?

RB: No, I feel like a survivor in a more literal sense. I am not dead. I say it like that because many of my friends have died, from armed revolutionary struggle, drug overdose, or AIDS. Although some who survived are now illustrious and famous celebrities of Spanish letters.

HS/MB: Writers are always asked for their inspiration and today will not be an exception. Some are inspired more from life, while others more from literature.

RB: In what concerns me, both.

HS/MB: Notwithstanding that, you are an extremely literary writer—to put it one way.

A: Well, if I had to choose one of the two things, and God pray that I never have to choose, I would choose literature. If I were offered a great library or an Inter-Rail ticket to Vladivostok, I would keep the library, without the slightest doubt. Besides, with the library, my trip would be much longer.

HS/MB: Like Borges, you have lived through your reading.

RB: In one way or another, we're all anchored to the book. A library is a metaphor for human beings or what's best about human beings, the same way a concentration camp can be a metaphor for what is worst about them. A library is total generosity.

HS/MB: Nevertheless, literature is not purely a sanctuary for good sentiment. It is also a refuge for hatefulness and resentment.

RB: I accept that. But it's indisputable that there are good sentiments in it. I think Borges said that a good writer is normally a good person. It must have been Borges because he said practically everything.

Good writers who are bad people are the exception. I can think only of one.

HS/MB: Who?

RB: Louis-Ferdinand Céline, a great writer and son of a bitch. Just an abject human being. It's incredible that the coldest moments of his abjection are covered under an aura of nobility, which is only attributable to the power of words.

HS/MB: Between Latin American and Spanish writers, where is your literary brotherhood?

RB: Basically among the Latin Americans—but also among the Spaniards. I don't believe in the separation of Latin American and Spanish writers. We all inhabit the same language. At least I think I cross those frontiers. And in my generation there is a mixed nucleus of writers, Spaniards and Latin Americans, the same way they were mixed in another era of Modernism, possibly the most revolutionary movement in Spanish literature of this century. Because of his strength, I think someone like **Javier Marías** is forced to influence Latin American literature, and he does. He is a great writer. By the same token, young Spanish writers should be influenced by someone like **Rodrigo Rey Rosa** or **Juan Villoro**, two enormous writers. I am extraor-

Spanish novelist, critic, and columnist Javier Marías (b. 1951) is one of the most respected contemporary Spanish writers in the world. Eleven of his books have been translated into English, including the acclaimed "Your Face Tomorrow" series.

Rodrigo Rey Rosa (b. 1958) is a Guatemalan short story writer and novelist. Paul Bowles translated many of Rey Rosa's works into English.

A Mexican writer and journalist, Juan Villoro (b. 1956) was highly praised by Bolaño. In a television interview Bolaño claimed Villoro's work was "opening up the path of the new Spanish novel of the millennium." Currently no full English translations are available, but excerpts from *El Testigo* (2004) have appeared in various journals including *The Quarterly Conversation* and *Common Knowledge*. His short story "Among Friends" was published in the journal *n+1* (Issue 8).

A Spanish novelist and friend of Bolaño's, Enrique Vila-Matas (b. 1948) is a force in contemporary Spanish literature. He is the author of over twenty-five works. His novels have just begun to be translated to English, including *Bartleby & Co.* and *Montano's Malady*.

Spanish novelist and screenwriter, Belén Gopegui (b. 1940) has won many Spanish language literary awards for her fiction. An English translation of *The Scale of Maps* will be available in 2010.

Born in Italy, Victoria de Stefano (b. 1940) moved to Venezuela in 1946. She has authored a number of novels and essay collections. Her work is not currently available in English.

Writer of the Spanish Golden Age, Francisco de Quevedo (1580–1645) was a prominent poet and politician. Much of his work is concerned with wordplay and metaphor.

dinarily blessed by a photograph of all of us together, from this and that side of the Atlantic: Rey Rosa, Villoro, Marías, **Vila-Matas**, **Belén Gopegui**, **Victoria de Stefano**.

HS/MB: Is it disturbing to think we have read many of our gods (James, Stendhal, Proust) in translation, in second-hand versions? Is that literature? If we spin the matter around, it's possible we might end up concluding that words don't have an equivalent.

RB: I think they do. Furthermore, literature is not made from words alone. Borges says that there are untranslatable writers. I think he uses **Quevedo** as an example. We could add García Lorca and others. Notwithstanding that, a work like *Don Quijote* can resist even the worst translator. As a matter of fact, it can resist mutilation, the loss of numerous pages and even a shit storm. Thus, with everything against it—bad translation, incomplete and ruined—any version of *Quijote* would still have very much to say to a Chinese or an African reader. And that is literature. We may lose a lot along the way. Without a doubt. But perhaps that was its destiny. Come what may.

"READING IS ALWAYS MORE IMPORTANT THAN WRITING"

INTERVIEW BY CARMEN BOULLOSA,
TRANSLATED BY MARGARET CARSON

FIRST PUBLISHED IN *BOMB*,
BROOKLYN, WINTER 2002

Roberto Bolaño belongs to the most select group of Latin American novelists. Chile of the coup d'état, Mexico City in the 1970s, and the reckless youth of poets are some of his frequent subjects, but he also takes up other themes: César Vallejo's deathbed, the hardships endured by unknown authors, life at the periphery. Born in Chile in 1953, he spent his teenage years in Mexico and moved to Spain at the end of the Seventies. As a poet, he founded the Infrarealist movement with Mario Santiago. In 1999 he won the Rómulo Gallegos Prize, previously awarded to Gabriel García Márquez and Mario Vargas Llosa, for his novel *The Savage Detectives*, for which he also received the prestigious Herralde Prize.

A prolific writer, a literary animal who makes no concessions, Bolaño successfully combines the two basic instincts of a novelist: He is attracted to historical events, and he desires to correct them, to point out the errors. From Mexico he acquired a mythical paradise, from Chile the inferno of the real, and from Blanes, the town in northeast Spain where he now lives and works, he purges the sins of both. No other novelist has been able to convey the complexity of the megalopolis Mexico City has become, and no one has revisited the horrors of the coup d'état in Chile and the Dirty War with such mordant, intelligent writing.

To echo Bolaño's words, "reading is more important than writing." Reading Roberto Bolaño, for

According to Bolaño, the Argentine writer Adolfo Bioy Casares (1914–1999) wrote "the first and best fantastic novel in Latin America." He was close friends with Borges and married to the writer Silvina Ocampo. The collaborations between Bioy Casares and Borges were many and varied. In 1990 he was awarded the Cervantes Prize, the highest honor in Spanish-language literature. His major work is *The Invention of Morel* (1940).

Perhaps Bolaño's favorite author, Julio Cortázar (1914–1984) influenced scores of Latin American authors. Bolaño refers to him as simply "the best."

An early force in Spanish language literature, Teresa de la Parra (1889–1936) was the daughter of a Venezuelan diplomat. She was born in Paris and raised in Europe but returned to Venezuela when she was nineteen. Her major work, *Iphigenia* (1924), is a work of modernist realism.

example. If anyone thinks that Latin American literature isn't passing through a moment of splendor, a look through some of his pages would be enough to dispel that notion. With Bolaño, literature—that inexplicably beautiful bomb that goes off and as it destroys, rebuilds—should feel proud of one of its best creations.

Our conversation took place via e-mail between Blanes and my home in Mexico City in the fall of 2001.

CARMEN BOULLOSA: In Latin America, there are two literary traditions that the average reader tends to regard as antithetical, opposite—or frankly, antagonistic: the fantastic—**Adolfo Bioy Casares,** the best of **Cortázar,** and the realist—Vargas Llosa, **Teresa de la Parra.** Hallowed tradition tells us that the southern part of Latin America is home to the fantastic, while the northern part is the center of realism. In my opinion, you reap the benefits of both: Your novels and narratives are inventions—the fantastic—and a sharp, critical reflection of reality—realist. And if I follow this reasoning, I would add that this is because you have lived on the two geographic edges of Latin America, Chile and Mexico. You grew up on both edges. Do you object to this idea, or does it appeal to you? To be honest, I find it somewhat illuminating, but it also leaves me dissatisfied: The best, the greatest writers (including Bioy Casares and his antithesis, Vargas Llosa) always draw from these two traditions. Yet from the standpoint of the English-speaking North, there's a tendency to pigeonhole Latin American literature within only one tradition.

ROBERTO BOLAÑO: I thought the realists came from the south (by that, I mean the countries in the Southern Cone), and writers of the fantastic came from the middle and northern parts of Latin America—if you pay attention to these compartmentalizations, which you should never, under any circumstances, take seriously. Twentieth century Latin American literature has followed the impulses of imitation and rejection, and may continue to do so for some time in the twenty-first century. As a general rule, human beings either imitate or reject the great monuments, never the small, nearly invisible treasures. We have very few writers who have cultivated the fantastic in the strictest sense— perhaps none, because among other reasons, economic underdevelopment doesn't allow subgenres to flourish. Underdevelopment only allows for great works of literature. Lesser works, in this monotonous or apocalyptic landscape, are an unattainable luxury. Of course, it doesn't follow that our literature is full of great works—quite the contrary. At first the writer aspires to meet these expectations, but then reality—the same reality that has fostered

The Argentine poet and short story writer Silvina Ocampo (1903–1993) was an essential member of the avant-garde literary culture of Buenos Aires. She published her fantastic literature in *Sur*, an intellectual literary journal published in Buenos Aires by her sister, Victoria Ocampo. A selection of her works, *Leopoldina's Dream*, is available in English.

these aspirations—works to stunt the final product. I think there are only two countries with an authentic literary tradition that have at times managed to escape this destiny—Argentina and Mexico. As to my writing, I don't know what to say. I suppose it's realist. I'd like to be a writer of the fantastic, like Philip K. Dick, although as time passes and I get older, Dick seems more and more realist to me. Deep down—and I think you'll agree with me—the question doesn't lie in the distinction of realist/fantastic but in language and structures, in ways of seeing. I had no idea that you liked Teresa de la Parra so much. When I was in Venezuela people spoke a lot about her. Of course, I've never read her.

CB: Teresa de la Parra is one of the greatest women writers, or greatest writers, and when you read her you'll agree. Your answer completely supports the idea that the electricity surging through the Latin American literary world is fairly haphazard. I wouldn't say it's weak, because suddenly it gives off sparks that ignite from one end of the continent to the other, but only every now and then. But we don't entirely agree on what I consider to be the canon. All divisions are arbitrary, of course. When I thought about the south (the Southern Cone and Argentina), I thought about Cortázar, **Silvina Ocampo's** delirious stories, Bioy Casares, and Borges (when you're dealing with authors like these, rankings don't matter: There is no "number one," they're all equally important authors), and I thought about that short, blurry novel by **María Luisa Bombal**, *House of Mist* (whose fame was perhaps more the result of scandal—she killed her ex-lover). I would place Vargas Llosa and the great de la Parra in the northern camp. But then things become complicated, because as you move even further north you find Juan Rulfo, and **Elena Garro** with *A Solid Home* (1958) and *Recollections of Things to Come* (1963). All divisions are arbitrary: There is no realism without fantasy, and vice versa.

In your stories and novels, and perhaps also in your poems, the reader can detect the settling of scores (as well as homages paid), which are important building blocks in your narrative structure. I don't mean that your novels are written in code, but the key to your narrative chemistry may lie in the way you blend hate and love in the events you recount. How does Roberto Bolaño, the master chemist, work?

RB: I don't believe there are any more scores settled in my writing than in the pages of any other author's books. I'll insist at the risk of sounding pedantic (which I probably am, in any case), that when I write the only thing that interests me is the writing itself; that is, the form, the rhythm, the plot. I laugh at some attitudes, at some people, at certain activities and matters of importance, simply

Chilean author María Luisa Bombal's (1910–1980) work broke the dominant realism of the age with a fantastic and surreal style. Her major work, *House of Mist* (1947), is available in English translation.

Mexican playwright, novelist, short story writer, and essayist Elena Garro (1920–1998) combined the surreal and imaginary traditions of Latin American literature with those of the Latin American realists. She had a tumultuous marriage to Octavio Paz that ended in divorce.

because when you're faced with such nonsense, by such inflated egos, you have no choice but to laugh. All literature, in a certain sense, is political. I mean, first, it's a reflection on politics, and second, it's also a political program. The former alludes to reality— to the nightmare or benevolent dream that we call reality—which ends, in both cases, with death and the obliteration not only of literature, but of time. The latter refers to the small bits and pieces that survive, that persist; and to reason. Although we know, of course, that in the human scale of things, persistence is an illusion and reason is only a fragile railing that keeps us from plunging into the abyss. But don't pay any attention to what I just said. I suppose one writes out of sensitivity, that's all. And why do you write? You'd better not tell me—I'm sure your answer will be more eloquent and convincing than mine.

CB: Right, I'm not going to tell you, and not because my answer would be any more convincing. But I must say that if there is some reason why I don't write, it's out of sensitivity. For me, writing means immersing myself in a war zone, slicing up bellies, contending with the remains of cadavers, then attempting to keep the combat field intact, still alive. And what you call "settling scores" seems much fiercer to me in your work than in that of many other Latin American writers.

In the eyes of this reader, your laughter is much more than a gesture; it's far more corrosive—it's a demolition job. In your books, the inner workings of the novel proceed in the classic manner: A fable, a fiction draws the reader in and at the same time makes him or her an accomplice in pulling apart the events in the background that you, the novelist, are narrating with extreme fidelity. But let's leave that for now. No one who has read you could doubt your faith in writing. It's the first thing that attracts the reader. Anyone who wants to find something other than writing in a book—for example, a sense of belonging, or being a member of a certain club or fellowship—will find no satisfaction in your novels or stories. And when I read you, I don't look for history, the retelling of a more or less recent period in some corner of the world. Few writers engage the reader as well as you do with concrete scenes that could be inert, static passages in the hands of "realist" authors. If you belong to a tradition, what would you call it? Where are the roots of your genealogical tree, and in which direction do its branches grow?

RB: The truth is, I don't believe all that much in writing. Starting with my own. Being a writer is pleasant—no, pleasant isn't the word—it's an activity that has its share of amusing moments, but I know of other things that are even more amusing, amusing in the same way that literature is for me. Hold-

A sixteenth century poet, short story writer and soldier, Francisco de Aldana (1540–1578) was a favorite of Cervantes and an integral part of the Spanish Renaissance.

Spanish poet Jorge Manrique (1440–1479) is a major figure in Spanish literary history. *Stanzas about the Death of his Father* has been translated many times, including in an 1833 translation by Longfellow.

An immensely important and prolific poet, Sor Juana Inés de la Cruz (1651–1695) lived in Mexico under Spanish rule. Her work was overtly radical for her time. She was especially concerned with the education of women and is viewed as an early champion of feminism.

A Dominican friar born in Monterrey, Servando Teresa de Mier (1763–1827) was a prominent preacher and politician in pre-revolutionary Mexico. While exiled in Spain he wrote his seminal works and aided the cause of Mexican independence.

One of the first Hispanic writers to be read internationally, Pedro Henríquez Ureña (1884–1946) was a proponent of the power of language to incite social change. An academic and son of a Dominican president, he was one of the most important Latin American cultural theorists and historians of the twentieth century.

ing up banks, for example. Or directing movies. Or being a gigolo. Or being a child again and playing on a more or less apocalyptic soccer team. Unfortunately, the child grows up, the bank robber is killed, the director runs out of money, the gigolo gets sick and then there's no other choice but to write. For me, the word "writing" is the exact opposite of the word "waiting." Instead of waiting, there is writing. Well, I'm probably wrong—it's possible that writing is another form of waiting, of delaying things. I'd like to think otherwise. But, as I said, I'm probably wrong. As to my idea of a canon, I don't know, it's like everyone else's—I'm almost embarrassed to tell you, it's so obvious: **Francisco de Aldana, Jorge Manrique,** Cervantes, the chroniclers of the Indies, **Sor Juana Inés de la Cruz, Fray Servando Teresa de Mier, Pedro Henríquez Ureña, Rubén Darío, Alfonso Reyes,** Borges, just to name a few and without going beyond the realm of the Spanish language. Of course, I'd love to claim a literary past, a tradition, a very brief one, made up of only two or three writers (and maybe one single book), a dazzling tradition prone to amnesia, but on the one hand, I'm much too modest about my work and on the other, I've read too much (and too many books have made me happy) to indulge in such a ridiculous notion.

CB: Doesn't it seem arbitrary to name as your literary ancestors authors who wrote exclusively in

Spanish? Do you include yourself in the Hispanic tradition, in a separate current from other languages? If a large part of Latin American literature (especially prose) is engaged in a dialogue with other traditions, I would say this is doubly true in your case.

RB: I named authors who wrote in Spanish in order to limit the canon. Needless to say, I'm not one of those nationalist monsters who only reads what his native country produces. I'm interested in French literature, in Pascal, who could foresee his death, and in his struggle against melancholy, which to me seems more admirable now than ever before. Or the utopian naiveté of Fourier. And all the prose, typically anonymous, of courtly writers (some Mannerists and some anatomists) that somehow leads to the endless caverns of the Marquis de Sade. I'm also interested in American literature of the 1880s, especially Twain and Melville, and the poetry of Emily Dickinson and Whitman. As a teenager, I went through a phase when I only read Poe. Basically, I'm interested in Western literature, and I'm fairly familiar with all of it.

CB: You only read Poe? I think there was a very contagious Poe virus going around in our generation—he was our idol, and I can easily see you as an infected teenager. But I'm imagining you as a

The most famous and acclaimed Nicaraguan poet, Rubén Darío (1867–1916) is credited with bringing modernism to Latin American literature.

A massive figure in Mexican culture in the first half of the twentieth century, Alfonso Reyes (1889–1959) was a prolific essayist, poet, and diplomat. He served as secretary of the Mexican embassy in Spain, minister to France, and ambassador to Brazil and Argentina. In 1943 he co-founded El Colegio Nacional in Mexico City. His major works include *The Position of America and Other Essays* (1950) and *Mexico in a Nutshell and Other Essays* (1964).

poet, and I want to turn to your narratives. Do you choose the plot, or does the plot chase after you? How do you choose—or how does the plot choose you? And if neither is true, then what happens? Pinochet's adviser on Marxism, the highly respected Chilean literary critic you baptize Sebastián Urrutia Lacroix, a priest and member of the Opus Dei, or the healer who practices Mesmerism, or the teenage poets known as the Savage Detectives—all these characters of yours have an historical counterpart. Why is that?

RB: Yes, plots are a strange matter. I believe, even though there may be many exceptions, that at a certain moment a story chooses you and won't leave you in peace. Fortunately, that's not so important—the form, the structure, always belong to you, and without form or structure there's no book, or at least in most cases that's what happens. Let's say the story and the plot arise by chance, that they belong to the realm of chance, that is, chaos, disorder, or to a realm that's in constant turmoil (some call it apocalyptic). Form, on the other hand, is a choice made through intelligence, cunning and silence, all the weapons used by Ulysses in his battle against death. Form seeks an artifice; the story seeks a precipice. Or to use a metaphor from the Chilean countryside (a bad one, as you'll see): It's not that I don't like precipices, but I prefer to see them from a bridge.

CB: Women writers are constantly annoyed by this question, but I can't help inflicting it on you—if only because after being asked it so many times, I regard it as an inevitable, though unpleasant ritual: How much autobiographical material is there in your work? To what extent is it a self-portrait?

RB: A self-portrait? Not much. A self-portrait requires a certain kind of ego, a willingness to look at yourself over and over again, a manifest interest in what you are or have been. Literature is full of autobiographies, some very good, but self-portraits tend to be very bad, including self-portraits in poetry, which at first would seem to be a more suitable genre for self-portraiture than prose. Is my work autobiographical? In a sense, how could it not be? Every work, including the epic, is in some way autobiographical. In the *Iliad* we consider the destiny of two alliances, of a city, of two armies, but we also consider the destiny of Achilles and Priam and Hector, and all these characters, these individual voices, reflect the voice, the solitude, of the author.

CB: When we were young poets, teenagers, and shared the same city (Mexico City in the seventies), you were the leader of a group of poets, the Infrarealists, which you've mythologized in your novel *The Savage Detectives*. Tell us a little about what poetry meant for the Infrarealists, about the Mexico City of the Infrarealists.

A poet and old friend of Bolaño's, Mario Santiago (1953–1998) was a member of Bolaño's inner circle and one of the founding members, along with Bolaño and others, of the infrarrelismo movement of the 1970s. Bolaño immortalized Santiago in *The Savage Detectives* as the Visceral Realist Ulises Lima.

RB: Infrarealism was a kind of Dada á la Mexicana. At one point there were many people, not only poets, but also painters and especially loafers and hangers-on, who considered themselves Infrarealists. Actually there were only two members, **Mario Santiago** and me. We both went to Europe in 1977. One night, in Rosellón, France, at the Port-Vendres train station (which is very close to Perpignan), after having suffered a few disastrous adventures, we decided that the movement, such as it was, had come to an end.

CB: Maybe it ended for you, but it remained vividly alive in our memories. Both of you were the terrors of the literary world. Back then I was part of a solemn, serious crowd—my world was so disjointed and shapeless that I needed something secure to hold onto. I liked the ceremonial nature of poetry readings and receptions, those absurd events full of rituals that I more or less adhered to, and you were the disrupters of these gatherings. Before my first poetry reading in Gandhi bookstore, way back in 1974, I prayed to God—not that I really believed in God, but I needed someone to call upon—and begged: Please, don't let the Infrarealists come. I was terrified to read in public, but the anxiety that arose from my shyness was nothing compared to the panic I felt at the thought that I'd be ridiculed: Halfway through the reading, the Infras might burst in and call me an idiot. You were there to convince the literary world that we shouldn't take ourselves so seriously over work that wasn't legitimately serious—and that with poetry (to contradict your Chilean saying) the precise point was to throw yourself off a precipice. But let me return to Bolaño and his work. You specialize in narratives—I can't imagine anyone calling your novels "lyrical"—and yet you're also a poet, an active poet. How do you reconcile the two?

RB: **Nicanor Parra** says that the best novels are written in meter. And Harold Bloom says that the best poetry of the twentieth century is written in prose. I agree with both. But on the other hand I find it difficult to consider myself an active poet. My understanding is that an active poet is someone who writes poems. I sent my most recent ones to you and I'm afraid they're terrible, although of course, out of kindness and consideration, you lied. I don't know. There's something about poetry. Whatever the case, the important thing is to keep reading it. That's more important than writing it, don't you think? The truth is, reading is always more important than writing.

A Chilean poet born in 1914, Nicanor Parra greatly influenced Bolaño's poetry and early fiction writings. Considered modernist, Parra's language resembles the much later work of the American Beat poets. Bolaño considered him "the best living Spanish language poet." A collection of his work *Antipoems: How to Look Better & Feel Great* is available in English.

"POSITIONS ARE POSITIONS AND SEX IS SEX"

INTERVIEW BY ELISEO ÁLVAREZ

FIRST PUBLISHED IN *TURIA*, BARCELONA, JUNE 2005

ELISEO ÁLVAREZ: Did your parents influence your love of literature, books?

ROBERTO BOLAÑO: No. In terms of genealogy, the truth is I come from two families: one that dragged with it 500 years of constant and rigorous illiteracy and the other, maternal, that dragged with it 300 years of laziness, just as constant and as rigorous. In that sense I'm the black sheep of the family. I suppose that they would have preferred any other thing. The truth is I'm fifty years old and knowing what I know now I wouldn't want my child to be a writer either. That isn't to say I would want him to continue with 500 more years of illiteracy, but why not 300 more years of laziness? It's quite hard to be a writer, although, let's not exaggerate. My mother read some books, and my father read Westerns occasionally. He read those little novels that are made to keep in your back pocket, because there was no television. My mother did read more, but if I had formed my mother's tastes I'd be a **Marcelo Serrano**- or **Isabel Allende**-type today. On the other hand, that wouldn't be so bad because I wouldn't have known the troubles of a writer but I would have known sweet millions, which seen with perspective is not a bad exit.

EA: It would be ideal to get a mix of both.

Chilean author Marcela Serrano (b. 1951) is a standard bearer of new Latin American fiction. Her major works include *Nosotras que nos queremos tanto* (1991) and *Para que no me olvides* (1994). Her translated works include *Antigua and My Life Before* (2001).

Perhaps the most famous female Chilean author, Isabel Allende (b. 1942) is an extremely prolific part of the magical realism movement. Bolaño considered her work "bad, but it's alive. It's anemic, like many Latin American authors, but it's alive." Her major works have been translated into English and include *The House of Spirits* (1982) and *Paula* (1995).

RB: I think a good mix is very difficult to obtain, especially for people of my generation, because we were very radical and we believed the sooner we got to the limit the better, and that's how it went for us.

EA: How did you discover reading?

RB: Surely because I was a very sensible kid, a very sensible adolescent. My father was a courier. He was also a professional heavyweight boxing champion in southern Chile. The only thing fit to do before that man was to be stronger than him—otherwise it was to opt for homosexuality. If he had depended on me, I would have opted for homosexuality, which seems to me a magnificent aesthetic escape, but it wouldn't have been natural. I'm heterosexual. So all that was left was film and books, and from childhood I dedicated myself to watching lots of film and reading lots of books basically and, evidently, trying to kill my father. Of course my father has always loved me very much, like all fathers. Now my son intends to kill me. I'll be the first to tell him: Kill me, son. Here is my neck. It's like the joke about the Jewish mother: In a fit of madness, the son cuts off his mother's head, flees, then stumbles, and while he's stumbling—with his mother's head still in his arms—the head says, "Son, are you all right?" A father's love for his son is similar. I suppose that within his brutality and his courage—he is a very courageous man—my father loved me as I love my son. In the end, one could talk for hours about the relationship between a father and a son. The only clear thing is that a father has to be willing to be spat upon by his son as many times as the son wishes to do it. Even still the father will not have paid a tenth of what he owes because the son never asked to be born. If you brought him into this world, the least you can do is put up with whatever insult he wants to offer.

EA: Do you agree with those who say that a child leaving the house is life's happiest and most dramatic moment?

RB: I don't agree with that. If it were up to me, I'd live to 100 and always protect my child. I don't think reason has anything to do with parent-children relationships, not at all. Perhaps from the perspective of a child, reason does impose itself, but from the perspective of a parent, it's very difficult to impose reason. One acts viscerally, in accordance with accumulation of fear and anguish. For example, when I was not yet a father, it was very difficult to injure me. I thought that I had finally acquired a type of invulnerability. But that all changed the moment my older child was born; that is to say, all of the fears and terrors I experienced as an adolescent re-emerged and duplicated, multiplied themselves by

100. See, I can put up with them myself, but I do not want my child to have to go through them. It's frightening, and now I have a daughter besides. I won't say anymore. I'll start to cry. The only explanation I could give would be to start to cry. It's beyond the beyond.

EA: Your family left for Mexico when you were fifteen-years old. Why?

RB: Basically, my mother had been to Mexico a couple of times and was familiar with the country and she convinced my father. My mother has always been an anxious person. She convinced my father that the best thing to do was to leave Chile and to go to Mexico. My parents were always separating and getting back together. Their relationship was stormy throughout my childhood and in a way Mexico was a small paradise, a place where they could start over. It was fun for them at first, although no fun at all for me. On the first day of school in Mexico, some guy challenged me to a fight just because I happened to be Chilean; we hadn't said a word to each other. He was a Mexican kid who didn't know how to fight very well and was short besides. I was certain that with two punches I could knock him to the ground, but I realized that if I knocked him down all the others would come after me and that's when I got smart: I grasped the situation in the act, and I directed the fight to a tie. I came off very well and he made good friends with me and no one ever wanted to fight me again. It was like a baptism in Aztec thought, quite disagreeable, but I realized where the shots were heading and the underlying message of the fight.

EA: Mexico was as dynamic as Chile was on its way to being when you arrived.

RB: Mexico was of a different dynamism. Look, in that era, Mexico City had 14 million inhabitants and it was a separate planet, it was the city where everything was possible. For me, because I came from a small town in Chile, a southern town besides, I exchanged a small town for a metropolis. I was never a resident of Santiago; I was born in Santiago, but I never lived in Santiago. I knew Santiago only from visiting.

EA: What were the strongest differences? The ones that cost you the most to get used to.

RB: Very few. Mexicans are really very hospitable. Since I was only fifteen-years old, I quickly Mexicanized myself. I felt totally Mexican. I never felt like a stranger in Mexico, except for that first day in school. There wasn't anything I had trouble getting used to.

EA: How did you arrive at Trotskyism?

RB: Just by being a contrarian I think. I did not like the priestly, clerical unanimity of the Communists. I've always been a leftist and I wasn't going to turn right just because I didn't like the Communist clergymen, so I became a Trotskyite. The problem is, once among the Trotskyites, I didn't like their clerical unanimity either, so I ended up being an anarchist. I was the only anarchist I knew and thank God, because otherwise I would have stopped being an anarchist. Unanimity pisses me off immensely. Whenever I realize that the whole world agrees on something, whenever I see that the whole world is cursing something in chorus, something rises to the surface of my skin that makes me reject it. They're probably infantile traumas. I don't see it as something that makes me proud.

EA: That's curious, because from what you're saying, unanimity is what was missing from your home.

RB: There was never any unanimity in my home. Not ever.

EA: How did you see the experiment with the socialism of the Chilean way?

RB: When I returned to Chile, shortly before the

coup, I believed in armed resistance, I believed in permanent revolution. I believed it existed then. I came back ready to fight in Chile and to continue fighting in Peru, in Bolivia.

EA: Allende must have seemed like a conservative grandpa to you guys.

RB: To us, in those years, Allende was a conservative. What happened is that his figure, in what concerns me, has changed vastly over time. I remember September 11, 1973: in one moment, I'm waiting to receive weapons to go and fight and I hear Allende say, in his speech no less, "Go forward knowing that, sooner rather than later, the great avenues will open again and free men will walk through them to construct a better society." In that moment, it seemed terrible to me, almost like a betrayal committed by Allende against those of us young people who were willing to fight for him. With time, that's one of the things that has ennobled Allende: saving us from death, accepting death for himself but saving us from it. I think that has made him huge in an immense way.

EA: But they detained you.

RB: I was detained, but a month and a half later in the south. The other thing happened in Santiago.

EA: And friends from school helped you escape.

RB: Friends from high school. I was detained for eight days, although a little while ago in Italy, I was asked, "What happened to you? Can you tell us a little about your half a year in prison?" That's due to a misunderstanding in a German book where they had me in prison for half a year. At first they sentenced me to less time. It's the typical Latin American tango. In the first book edited for me in Germany, they give me one month in prison; in the second book—seeing that the first one hadn't sold so well—they raise it to three months; in the third book I'm up to four months; in the fourth book it's five. The way it's going, I should still be a prisoner now.

EA: Did you have doubts about being able to make a living as a writer?

RB: I had many doubts. In fact I worked at other things. Economic doubts for many years, always economic; never vocational. What interested me, at twenty years old, more than writing poetry, because I also wrote poetry (in reality, I only wrote poetry), what I wanted was to live like a poet, even though today I wouldn't be able to specify what it meant to me to live like a poet. Anyway my basic interest was to live like a poet. For me, being a poet meant being revolutionary and completely open to all cultural manifestations, all sexual expressions, in the end, being open to every experience with drugs. Tolerance meant—much more than tolerance, a word we didn't much like—universal brotherhood, something totally utopian.

EA: Doesn't prose make that sensibility more profound?

RB: Prose has always demanded more work. We were against work. Among other things, we were tirelessly lazy. There wasn't a single person who could make us work. I worked only when I didn't have any other choice. Also, we accepted living life with very little. We were complete Spartans, with meager means, but at the same time we were Athenians and sodomites enjoying all aspects of life, poor but luxurious. This was all related to the hippies, the North American model, May of '68 in Europe, to many things in the end.

EA: Do you owe your sentimental education to Mexico?

RB: More than anything I owe Mexico my intellectual education. My sentimental education? I owe that more to Spain, I think. When I came to Spain, I was twenty-three or twenty-four years old. I arrived thinking I was already a man—through and through—and that I knew everything there was to know about sex, and for me a sentimental education is almost synonymous with a sexual education. In reality, I knew nothing, which I quickly realized with the first girl I met. I knew many positions, but positions are positions and sex is sex.

EA: It's one thing to know methodology—

RB: Exactly. My sentimental education begins at age twenty-three in Europe.

EA: Have you not wanted to return to Mexico for fear of finding a completely different country from the one you left and having lost your connection?

RB: Yes, that's true. But it's also true that, although I've traveled a lot, I don't recognize many countries from afar, and between getting to know a new country and returning to Mexico, a country I love but which is swarmed by ghosts, among them the ghost of my dead best friend, and where I believe I would have a very bad time, I prefer to go to other places. I've gotten too comfortable to go around choosing to spend a bad time in a particular place. I used to love to go to places where I knew I'd have a bad time. But, now, for what?

EA: Were you an anarchist when you arrived in Spain?

RB: Yes. I found many fellow anarchists and I started to cease being one myself. How did it occur to them? What kind of anarchy was that?

EA: In Spain, the people were coming out from under a dictatorship, and they had the power.

RB: Yes. The trouble is that in Barcelona I didn't just find Catalan people, who I found to be magnificent, but also people from everywhere in Spain and Europe and South America too. There were people who had come from all over the world, above all from the West, to understand us. One lived very well. There was work. In 1977 and '78 there were jobs that paid very little but that allowed you to subsist. State pressures had started to relax. Spain had begun to be a democratic country and there were wide margins of liberty. For a foreigner like me, that was a gift for which I will endlessly be grateful.

EA: Did you already believe that Chilean literature revolved around Pablo Neruda?

RB: I thought that even before. The problem is that this isn't exactly how it is. For me, Chile's great poet is Nicanor Parra and after Nicanor Parra there are several others. Neruda is one of them, without a doubt. Neruda is what I pretended to be at age twenty: living like a poet without writing. Neruda wrote three very good books; the rest—the great majority—are very bad, some truly infected. But he already lived like a poet and not just like a poet: he performed like a sun poet, like a poet king.

Born in 1914, Octavio Paz is one of Mexico's most important writers and the winner of the 1990 Nobel Prize for Literature. He has been outspoken in the realm of Mexican politics and served as the Mexican ambassador to India from 1962–1968.

One of the most prolific and outspoken writers in twentieth century Spanish language literature, Carlos Fuentes (b. 1928) was also one of the first modern Spanish language writers to garner real success in the United States. Born in Panama City, Panama, Fuentes was also steeped in the magical realism movement. His 1985 novel *Gringo Viejo* was adapted into a Hollywood film.

EA: The thing that happened with Neruda—the type of man who appeared to be against the establishment but then lives off the state—hasn't that happened with many Mexican writers? Let's use **Octavio Paz** and **Carlos Fuentes** as examples.

RB: It's because in literature, the only country where this doesn't happen, at least from what I can tell, is Argentina. What happens in Mexico happens in all of the other countries in Latin America; in Chile a little bit less but it happens there as well. In Argentina, there is a level of professionalism expected of writers and that the state tries to ignore, but in other countries it is asked of writers that they be independent yet also that they charge the state, which reminds one of a phrase from Mexico's President Echeverría, who said, "neither to the right, nor to the left, nor in a static center, but onward and upward." If the writer can't ask the state for money, he gets mad and will protest the lack of help using his platform like the profoundly independent writer that he is. Besides, that type of direct help translates into all kinds of cultural advances, including jobs.

EA: Are you more on the side of the Mexicanness of Paz or the universalism of Fuentes?

RB: I think Octavio Paz is more universal. The truth is, until the moment I lived in Mexico, Fuentes and Paz were, as one would say in Spain, "*a partir un piñon*," intimate friends. One was the tsar and the other the tsarevitch; they were very fond of one another. I would guess that Fuentes even loved Paz, if it's possible for Fuentes to love someone, which is another topic; and Paz probably loved Fuentes, if Paz has ever loved anyone, which is again another topic. Evidently, I don't side with either of them.

EA: This thing with intellectuals saying things to one another, it's quite Mexican.

RB: It depends on what's being said. Yes, it's not unusual in Mexico. Intellectual life—artistic life—in Mexico is very active, as are all aspects of life in Mexico. Mexico is a tremendously vital country, despite the fact that, paradoxically, it's the country where death is the most present. Perhaps being that vital is what keeps death so close. I feel as distant from Fuentes as I do from Paz. I recognize the writer in Paz, above all, in his essays. He is more interesting as a prose writer than Fuentes is as a prose writer. As a poet, there are four poems by Paz that I could still reread without losing interest, there's even one I still like a lot. The truth is, in general, Mexican poetry tends toward pride, toward starchiness, although there are notable exceptions evidently. There is Mexican poetry I like very much. I like **López Velarde** a lot, I like **Tablada**; among the

Considered one of the fathers of modern Mexican poetry, Ramón López-Velarde (1888–1921) was beloved in his country yet garnered little attention outside its borders. Writing during the Mexican Revolution and the turmoil of the years after, he had a profound effect on a generation of Mexican writers. A collection of his work, *Song of the Heart: Selected Poems by Ramon López-Velarde*, is available in English.

Mexican poet, novelist, and playwright José Juan Tablada (1871–1945) left Mexico in 1914 for the United States. His polemical and satirical writings during the Mexican Revolution angered many important politicians and military officials. Choosing exile, he spent time in Texas, New York City, and Japan. He is credited with introducing the haiku to Spanish-language literature.

An icon in Argentine metaphysical literature, Macedonio Fernández (1874–1952), known to most as simply "Macedonio," was a mentor to the young Jorge Luis Borges. An English translation of his novel *The Museum of Eterna's Novel* will be available in 2010.

An Argentine writer, professor, and literary critic, Ricardo Piglia (b. 1941) is one of the foremost authorities on Latin American literature. Author of several novels and short story collections, he has been a professor at the University of Buenos Aires, the University of California at Davis, and Princeton. His English works include *Artificial Respiration* (1980) and *Money to Burn* (1997)

An Argentine painter of European descent, Xul Solar (1887–1963) was a key member of the avant-garde movement in Buenos Aires in the 1920's. Spending the years 1912–1924 in Europe, Solar's return to Argentina in 1924 found a burgeoning artistic movement eager to combine the Argentine avant-garde with that of Continental Europe. Solar had a deep affinity for language, which led him to create several of his own languages and work on the creation of an international language.

modern writers I like Mario Santiago, who was my friend. But, look, back to your question, if I had to sit near one of them, I'd sit closer to Octavio Paz than to Fuentes.

EA: Must we speak of **Macedonio** in order to speak of Borges?

RB: Piglia believes so; I don't. Piglia believes that Macedonio is very important. Macedonio seems to me to be very important, but I think he is important only as measured by his proximity to Borges. In fact, Borges illuminates a ton of writers and painters. For example, **Xul Solar**, who, if it weren't for Borges, would probably only be known in Argentina. Perhaps Solar's paintings deserve only to be known in Argentina, but by being touched by Borges, through the Borgian experience, they become paintings that transcend the limits of Argentina. I think Xul was capable of seducing anyone; he was a very seductive type. And Macedonio seduces Borges perhaps by his courage. Borges is a man who loves courage, who looks for it in people and who knows how to appreciate it besides, and I believe Macedonio is one of those writers, one of the most courageous beings Borges knows. He is a man truly without duplicity. Borges knows he can always rely on Macedonio and if there were ever a moment when that wouldn't be possible, he knows he would hear it directly from Macedonio himself. Macedonio, the Borgian Macedonio that comes to us through Borges' prose at least, incarnates the ideal Argentine, he makes possible the impossible Argentine, the Argentine with a little Creole in him, who lives for many years in a little room, who is a Spartan in his habits, the man who is always mourning over a woman, which is something that seduces Borges, something that would seduce anyone of this era. Because it isn't just Borges who is head over heals for Macedonio, there are a ton of writers of Borges' generation who are awestruck by him. Borges was awestruck by those Creole things of his, because he was a Creole who left in order to speak of Schopenhauer, and speak well besides. He was of an exquisite logic. But, for me, what's important is Borges.

EA: Soon *Nazi Literature in Latin America* comes out.

RB: ...*in the Americas*. It's the whole continent. There are several North American authors, I assure you.

EA: I'm convinced.

RB: It's just that I've seen it written as *Nazi Literature in Latin America*, not *Nazi Literature in the*

Argentine author, critic, and translator Juan Rodolfo Wilcock (1919–1978) spent time working at nearly every major Latin American literary magazine. His work *The Temple of the Iconoclasts*, available in English, was a seminal text for Bolaño. He claims "buy it, steal it, borrow it, but read it."

Americas. The trouble is that there aren't any Canadian authors. I had a Quebecker in mind but they were cut in the end for lack of merit.

EA: Is there a Cervantean influence in this book?

RB: I think all writers who write in Spanish have or should have a Cervantean influence. We are all indebted to Cervantes, in large or small part, but we are all indebted. The genealogy for *Nazi Literature in the Americas* does not come from there. This book, I'll give it to you in descending order, owes a lot to *The Temple of Iconoclasts* by **Rodolfo Wilcock**, who is an Argentine writer but who wrote the book in Italian.

EA: He's almost a cult writer.

RB: It's just that he is an exceptional writer; he is a major writer. He is a writer who, I think, has done nothing but grow since death. Wilcock keeps growing. At the same time, his book *The Temple of Iconoclasts* itself owes a debt to *A Universal History of Infamy* by Borges, which is not surprising at all because Wilcock was a friend and admirer of Borges. Borges' *A Universal History of Infamy*, too, owes a debt to one of his teachers, Alfonso Reyes, the Mexican writer who has a book I think called *Real and Imagined Portraits*—my memory is in torpor. It's just a jewel. Alfonso Reyes' book also owes a debt to **Marcel Schwob's** *Imaginary Lives*, which is where this all comes from. But at the same time, *Imaginary Lives* owes a major debt to the methodology and form of certain biographies perused by encyclopedic types. Those are the uncles, parents and godparents of my book, I think, which is without a doubt the worst of the bunch, but there you have it anyway.

The French author Marcel Schwob (1867–1905) was a precursor to the surrealists. His major work is *Imaginary Lives* (1896).

EA: Following the enormous critical impact *The Savage Detectives* had, were you certain then you were going to dedicate yourself to this forever?

RB: No, I had been certain before—certain in the economic sense—that I could live from literature, as a matter of fact I had been certain years before. I started to live from literature starting in 1992 and *Savage Detectives* was published in 1998. Starting in 1992, which coincides with a grave illness, my income has been exclusively gained from literature.

EA: There is a general contempt that writers have toward critics, but you ask for improvement from criticism.

RB: Literary criticism is a discipline that represents something more for me than literature. Literature is prose, novel and short story, dramaturgy, poetry, and literary essays and literary criticism. Above all, I think it is necessary that there be literary criticism—without accident—in our countries, not ten lines about an author the critic will probably never read again. That is to say, it's necessary to have criticism that mends the literary landscape along the way.

EA: I know many book jacket critics.

RB: I've practiced literary criticism myself, and one could say a lot about that.

EA: Within mass media, there is a tendency to limit the importance of genre.

RB: Perhaps, but I think it is very important. I view criticism as a literary creation, not just as the bridge that unites the reader with the writer. Literary critics, if they do not assume themselves to be the reader, are also throwing everything overboard. The interesting thing about literary critics, and that is where I ask for creativity from literary criticism, creativity at all levels, is that he assumes himself to be the reader, an endemic reader capable of arguing a reading, of proposing diverse readings, like something completely different from what criticism tends to be, which is like an exegesis or a diatribe. For me, Harold Bloom is an example of a notable critic, although I am generally in disagreement with him and even enraged by him, but I like to read him. Or Steiner: The French have a very long tradition of very creative critics and essayists who are very good, who illuminate not just one work but a whole era of literature, sometimes committing grave mistakes, but us narrators and writers also commit errors.

EA: One of your characters says, "One has the moral obligation to be responsible for one's actions and for one's words but also for one's silence."

RB: One of my characters says that? It sounds so good it hardly seems written by me.

EA: Is that also fair to say about writers?

RB: No, for writers that isn't fair, but without a doubt, in predetermined moments, yes. If I'm walking down the street and see a pedophile molesting a kid and I stop and silently stare, not only am I responsible for my silence but I am also a complete son of a bitch. However, there is a certain type of silence in which—

EA: Are there literary silences?

RB: Yes, there are literary silences. Kafka's, for example, which is a silence that cannot be. When he

For more on Juan Rulfo,
see page 43.

asks that his papers be burned, Kafka is opting for silence, opting for a literary silence, all in a literary era. That is to say, he was completely moral. Kafka's literature, aside from being the best work, the highest literary work of the twentieth century, is of an extreme morality and of an extreme gentility, things that usually do not go together either.

EA: And what of **Rulfo's** silence?

RB: Rulfo's silence, I think, is obedient to something so quotidian that explaining it is a waste of time. There are several versions: One told by Monterroso is that Rulfo had an uncle so-and-so who told him stories and when Rulfo was asked why he didn't write anymore, his answer was that his uncle so-and-so had died. And I believe it too. Another explanation is simple and natural and it is that everything has an expiration date. For example I am much more worried about Rimbaudian silence than I am about Rulfian silence. Rulfo stopped writing because he had already written everything he wanted to write and *because* he sees himself incapable of writing anything better, he simply stops. Rimbaud would probably have been able to write something much better, which is to say bringing his words up even higher, but his is a silence that raises questions for Westerners. Rulfo's silence doesn't raise questions; it's a close silence, quotidian. After desert, what the hell are you going to eat? There is a third literary silence—one doesn't seek it—of the shade which one is sure was there under the threshold and which has never been made tangible. There stands the silence of Georg Büchner for example. He died at twenty-five or twenty-four years of age, he leaves behind three or four stage plays, masterworks. One of them is *Woyzeck*, an absolute masterwork. Another is about the death of Danton, which is an enormous masterwork, not absolute but quite notable. The other two—one is called *Leonce y Lena*, I can't remember the other one—are fundamentally important. All before he turned twenty-five. What might have happened had Büchner not died; what kind of writer might he have been? The kind of silence that isn't sought out is the silence of...I do not dare call it destiny...a manifestation of impotence. The silence of death is the worst kind of silence, because Rulfian silence is accepted and Rimbaudian silence is sought, but the silence of death is the one that cuts the edge off what could have been and never will be, that which we will never know. We'll never know if Büchner would have been bigger than Goethe. I think so, but we'll never know. We'll never know what he might have written at age thirty. And that extends across the whole planet like a stain, an atrocious illness that in one way or another puts our habits in check, our most ingrained certainties.

THE LAST INTERVIEW

INTERVIEW BY MÓNICA MARISTAIN

PLAYBOY, MEXICO EDITION, JULY 2003

In the blurry panorama of Spanish-language literature, a place where young writers each day seem more preoccupied with obtaining scholarships and plum posts at various consulates than contributing to artistic expression, the figure of a lean man stands out, blue backpack at the ready, enormously framed eyeglasses, a never-ending cigarette between his fingers and, whenever there is a shortage, sharp, blunt wit.

Roberto Bolaño, born in Chile in 1953, is the best thing to happen to the writing profession in a long time. Since becoming famous and pocketing the Herralde (1998) and Rómulo Gallegos (1999) prizes for his monumental *The Savage Detectives*, perhaps the great Mexican novel of our time, his influence and stature have grown steadily: Everything he says, with his pointed sense of humor, his exquisite intelligence, and everything he writes, with a sure pen, great poetic risk and profound creative commitment, is worthy of the attention of those who admire and, of course, those who detest him.

The author, who turns up as a character in the novel *Soldiers of Salamis* by Javier Cercas and is paid homage in Jorge Volpi's last novel, *An End to Madness*, is a divider of opinions, like all brilliant men, and a generator of bitter antipathy, despite his tender good nature. His voice is somewhere between high-pitched and hoarse, and like any good Chilean, the one with which he responds is always courteous. He will not write one story more until finishing his next novel, which will be about the murder of countless women in Ciudad Juárez. He is already at 900 pages and not finished yet.

Bolaño lives in Blanes, Spain, and he's very sick. He hopes that a liver transplant will give him the strength to live with the same intensity worshipped by those fortunate enough to address him in private. His friends say he sometimes forgets about his doctor's visits because he's writing.

At fifty years old, Bolaño has crisscrossed Latin America as a backpacker, escaped the clutches of Pinochet because one of his jailers was a classmate in school, lived in Mexico (a section of Bucareli Street will someday bear his name), got to know Farabundo Martí's militants before they assassinated the poet Roque Dalton in El Salvador, kept watch over a Catalonian campground and sold costume jewelry in Europe. Also, he always stole good books because reading is not just a matter of posturing. He has transformed the course of Latin American literature. And he has done it without warning and without asking permission, the way Juan García Madero, adolescent antihero of his glorious *The Savage Detectives*, would have done: "I'm in my first semester of law school. I wanted to study literature, not law, but my aunt insisted and in the end I gave in. I'm an orphan and someday I'll be a lawyer. That's what I told my aunt and uncle, then I shut myself in my room and cried all night." The rest—the remaining pages of the novel—

has been compared to Julio Cortázar's *Hopscotch* and even Gabriel García Márquez's *One Hundred Years of Solitude*. In the face of such hyperbole, he might have said, "No way." Thus, on this occasion, let's get to what's important: the interview.

MÓNICA MARISTAIN: Were you blessed with a kind of courage in life by being born dyslexic?

ROBERTO BOLAÑO: Not at all. There were problems when I played soccer, I'm left-handed; problems when I masturbated, I'm left-handed; problems when I wrote, I'm right-handed. So, as you can see, no significant problems.

MM: Did Enrique Vila-Matas remain a friend after the fight you had with the organizers of the Rómulo Gallegos prize?

RB: My fight with the jury and the organizers of the prize was due basically to their expectation that I blindly endorse, from Blanes, their choice without having participated. Their methods, transmitted to me by phone by a Chavista pseudo-poet, too closely resembled the deterrent arguments of the Casa de las Américas (Cuba). It seemed to me that eliminating **Daniel Sada** or **Jorge Volpi** in the first round was an enormous mistake, for example. They said what I wanted was to travel with my wife and kids—something that was completely false. I

A well known Mexican writer, Daniel Sada (b. 1953) is the author of *Porque parece mentira, la verdad nunca se sabe* (1999), a hybrid work of epic poetry and novel. His short story "The Ominous Phenomenon" appeared in the English-language collection *Best of Contemporary Mexican Fiction* (2009).

A Mexican author who helped start the break from magical realism, Jorge Volpi (b. 1968) is best known for his novels and essays. His major work is *In Search of Klingsor* (1999).

A Mexican novelist who enjoys commercial success, Ángeles Mastretta (b. 1949) is best known for her strong female characters and social commentaries. To Bolaño she represented something of the old guard of Latin American literature. Her major works are available in English.

suppose that from my indignation over this lie, a letter surfaced in which I called them neo-Stalinists, among other things. In fact, I was informed that they intended, from the beginning, to reward another author, who wasn't Vila-Matas, whose novel seemed to me to be so good, and who without a doubt was one of my candidates.

MM: Why don't you have air-conditioning in your studio?

RB: Because my motto is "Et in Esparta ego," not "Et in Arcadia ego."

MM: Don't you think that had you gotten drunk with Isabel Allende and **Ángeles Mastretta**, someone else might be your double in terms of your books?

RB: I don't believe so, first of all, because those women avoid drinking with someone like me. Secondly, because I no longer drink. Thirdly, because not even in my worst drunkenness have I ever lost the minimum lucidity, a sense of prosody and rhythm, or a certain rejection in the presence of plagiarism, mediocrity and silence.

MM: What is the difference between a writer and an author?

RB: Silvina Ocampo is one example of an author.

Marcela Serrano is one example of a writer. You can measure light-years between one and the other.

MM: What makes you believe you're a better poet than narrator?

RB: The degree to which I blush when, by mere chance, I open one of my poetry or prose books. The poetry books make me less embarrassed.

MM: Are you Chilean, Spanish, or Mexican?

RB: I am Latin American.

MM: What is your motherland?

RB: I regret having to give a pretentious response. My children, Lautaro and Alexandra, are my only motherland. And perhaps, in the background, certain moments, certain streets, certain faces or scenes or books that are inside me and that some day I will forget—that is the best one can do for a motherland.

MM: What is Chilean literature?

RB: Likely the nightmares of the most resentful and gray poet, and perhaps the most cowardly of all Chilean poets: **Carlos Pezoa Véliz**, dead at the beginning of the 20th century and author of only two memorable poems, but truly memorable indeed,

Chilean poet Carlos Pezoa Véliz (1879–1908) embodies the melancholy at the core of Chilean and Latin American poetry. His style was clear and simple and, to Bolaño, appeared to be a direct representation of the Chilean people.

Spanish journalist and literary critic Ignacio Echevarría was a close friend of Bolaño's and became Bolaño's literary executor. He is currently a staff writer for *El País* in Madrid.

Another friend of Bolaño's, Rodrigo Fresán (b. 1963) is an Argentine fiction writer. His work *Gardens of Kensington*, 2006, was translated by Natasha Wimmer.

A prolific Spanish author, A.G. Porta was a close friend of Bolaño's. His debut, and most popular work, is *Consejos de un discípulo de Morrison a un fanático de Joyce seguido de Diario de Bar*, 1984, which was co-authored by Bolaño. None of his work is available in English.

A Chilean author, screenwriter, and director, Antonio Skármeta (b. 1940) has had his major works translated to English. The program to which Maristain is referring is a television program focusing on Spanish-language literature that was hosted by Skármeta.

A Spanish author, Javier Cercas (b. 1962) enjoys relative success in the English speaking world. His novels *The Soldiers of Salamis*, 2004, and *The Speed of Light*, 2007, are both available in English. One of the main characters in *The Soldiers of Salamis* is named "Roberto Bolaño."

who continues to suffer and dream of us. It's possible—isn't it?—that Pezoa Véliz is agonizing and has yet to die, and that his final minute has been rather long, and that we might all be inside of him. Or at least that all we Chileans are inside of him.

MM: Why do you always take the opposite view of things?

RB: I never take the opposite view of things.

MM: Do you have more friends than enemies?

RB: I have a sufficient amount of friends and enemies, all gratuitous.

MM: Who are your dearest friends?

RB: My best friend was the poet Mario Santiago, who died in 1998. At present, three of my best friends are **Ignacio Echevarría**, **Rodrigo Fresán** and **A.G. Porta**.

MM: Did **Antonio Skármeta** ever invite you on his program?

RB: One of his secretaries, perhaps his maid, called me on the phone once. I told her I was too busy.

MM: Did **Javier Cercas** share the royalties for *Soldiers of Salamis* with you?

RB: No, of course not.

MM: **Enrique Lihn, Jorge Teillier** or Nicanor Parra?

RB: Nicanor Parra above all, including Pablo Neruda and **Vicente Huidobro** and **Gabriela Mistral**.

MM: **Eugenio Montale**, T.S. Eliot, or **Xavier Villaurrutia?**

RB: Montale. If it had been James Joyce instead of Eliot, then Joyce. If it had been Ezra Pound instead of Eliot, then Pound without a doubt.

MM: John Lennon, Lady Di, or Elvis Presley?

RB: The Pogues. Or Suicide. Or Bob Dylan. Well, but let's not be pretentious: Elvis forever. Elvis and his golden voice, with a sheriff's badge, driving a Mustang and stuffing himself full of pills.

MM: Who reads more, you or Rodrigo Fresán?

RB: Depends. The West is for Rodrigo. The East is for me. Then we'll count the books in our corresponding areas and it might appear that we've read them all.

MM: In your opinion, what is Pablo Neruda's greatest poem?

Chilean born poet, playwright, and novelist Enrique Lihn (1929–1988) is the subject of a Bolaño short story, "Meeting with Enrique Lihn." Lihn's major works are available in English.

An important Chilean poet, Jorge Teillier (1935–1996) has had two collections of selected works translated into English, *In Order to Talk with the Dead*, 1993, and *From the Country of Nevermore*, 1990.

A major Chilean poet, Vicente Huidobro (1893–1948) was one of Bolaño's favorites. He was prolific, and selections of his work have been translated into English, including *Altazor*, his major work.

A Chilean poet, Gabriela Mistral (1889–1957) was the first Latin American to win the Nobel Prize for Literature. Her major works *Desolación* (1922), *Ternura* (1924), and *Tala* (1938) have been translated into English.

Eugenio Montale (1886–1981) was a Nobel Prize-winning Italian poet and translator.

Mexican poet, playwright, essayist, and critic Xavier Villaurrutia (1903–1950) was a significant Mexican literary figure. He is most widely appreciated for his work in the theatre, but his complete works, including poems, plays, and a novel have been translated into English.

RB: Almost any in *Residence on Earth*.

MM: If you had known Gabriela Mistral, what would you have told her?

RB: Forgive me, ma, I've been bad, but I turned good for the love of a woman.

MM: And to Salvador Allende?

RB: Little or nothing. Those who have power—even for a short time—know nothing about literature; they are solely interested in power. I can be a clown to my readers, if I damn well please, but never to the powerful. It sounds a bit melodramatic. It sounds like the statement of an honest whore. But in short, that's how it is.

MM: And to Vicente Huidobro?

RB: Huidobro bores me a little. He's excessively happy-go-lucky, too much like a descending skydiver belting songs from the Tyrol. Skydivers who descend while engulfed in flames are better, or those who fall flat, like the ones whose parachutes never open.

MM: Does Octavio Paz continue to be the enemy?

RB: For me, certainly not. I don't know what the poets who wrote like clones of his during that era, while I was living in Mexico, must think. It's been a long time since I've known anything about Mexican poetry. I reread José Juan Tablada and Ramón López Velarde; I can even recite "Sor Juana" divided in three, but I know nothing of what those who, like me, are nearing fifty years old write.

MM: Wouldn't you give that role to Carlos Fuentes today?

RB: It's been a long while since I've read anything by Carlos Fuentes.

MM: What do you make of the fact that **Arturo Pérez-Reverte** is the most widely read author in the Spanish language?

RB: Pérez-Reverte or Isabel Allende. It strikes me the same. **Feuillet** was the most widely read French author of his time.

MM: And of the fact that Arturo Pérez-Reverte has been admitted to the Royal Spanish Academy?

RB: The Royal Spanish Academy is a cave full of privileged craniums. **Juan Marsé** is not a member,

One of Europe's best-selling authors, Arturo Pérez-Reverte (b. 1951) is a Spanish novelist and former war correspondent. He is known for "Alatriste," a collection of novels based on the life and times of a seventeenth century Spanish soldier. The first four books in the series are available in English.

Octave Feuillet (1821–1890) was a French novelist and dramatist.

Juan Marsé (b. 1933) is an award-winning Spanish novelist, journalist, and screenwriter. His translated works include *Lizard Tails*, 2004, and *Shanghai Nights*, 2007.

Novelist, poet, and essayist, Juan Goytisolo (b. 1931) is one of the foremost modern Spanish authors.

One of contemporary Spain's most important writers, Eduardo Mendoza (b. 1943) has enjoyed mainstream success since the publication of his first novel *The Truth About the Savolta Case*, 1992.

Spanish poet, essayist, translator, and professor Olvido García Valdés (b. 1950) is one of the preeminent figures in Spanish intellectual life.

Spanish poet and novelist Álvaro Pombo (b. 1939) was awarded the 2006 Premio Planeta for his novel *La fortuna de Matilda Turpin*. His novels *The Hero of the Big House*, 1988, and *The Resemblance*, 1989, are available in English.

Chilean novelist, Diamela Eltit (b. 1949) is a former cultural attaché at the Chilean embassy in Mexico. Several of her novels are available in English, including *Custody of the Eyes*, 2005.

Juan Goytisolo is not a member, **Eduardo Mendoza** and Javier Marías are not members, **Olvido García Valdes** is not a member. I don't remember if **Álvaro Pombo** is a member (if he is, it's likely due to a misunderstanding), but Pérez-Reverte is a member. Besides, Coelho is a member of the Brazilian Academy of Letters.

MM: Do you regret having criticized the menu served by **Diamela Eltit**?

RB: I never criticized her menu. If anything, I would have criticized her sense of humor, that of a vegetarian, or better still, her sense of humor on a diet.

MM: Does it hurt that she considers you a bad person since the story of that spoiled dinner came out?

RB: No, poor thing. Diamela doesn't hurt me. Other things hurt me.

MM: Have you shed one tear about the widespread criticism you've drawn from your enemies?

RB: Lots and lots. Every time I read that someone has spoken badly of me I begin to cry, I drag myself across the floor, I scratch myself, I stop writing indefinitely, I lose my appetite, I smoke less, I engage in sport, I go for walks on the edge of the sea, which by the way is less than 30 meters from my house, and I ask the seagulls, whose ancestors ate the fish who ate Ulysses: Why me? Why? I've done you no harm.

MM: With regard to your work, whose opinion do you value most?

RB: My books are read by Carolina [wife], then [Jorge] Herralde [editor of *Anagrama*], and then I endeavor to forget them forever.

MM: What things did you buy with the prize money from the Rómulo Gallegos award?

RB: Not much, a suitcase as far as I can remember.

MM: During the time when you lived on literary competitions, was there a prize you couldn't claim?

RB: None. Spanish city halls, in this respect, are decent and beyond reproach.

MM: Were you a good waiter, or a better costume jewelry vendor?

RB: I have best redeemed myself as the night watchman of a campsite near Barcelona. Nobody ever stole while I was there. I stopped some fights that

An Italian film and stage actor, Vittorio Gassman (1922–2000) appeared in dozens of movies and theatrical productions.

could have ended badly, and I prevented a lynching—although on second thought, I should have lynched or strangled the guy myself.

MM: Have you experienced fierce hunger, bone-chilling cold, breathtaking heat?

RB: As **Vittorio Gassman** says in a film, "Modestly, yes."

MM: Have you stolen a book you later didn't like?

RB: Never. The good thing about stealing books—unlike safes—is that one can carefully examine their contents before perpetrating the crime.

MM: Have you ever walked in the middle of the desert?

RB: Yes, and one of those times on the arm of my grandmother. The elderly woman was tireless, and I didn't think we would make it.

MM: Have you seen colorful fish underwater?

RB: Of course. Without going further than Acapulco, in 1974 or 1975.

MM: Have you ever burned your skin with a cigarette?

RB: Never voluntarily.

MM: Have you ever carved the name of your beloved in the trunk of a tree?

RB: I have committed greater abuses, but let's draw the veil at that.

MM: Have you seen the most beautiful woman in the world?

RB: Yes, sometime around 1984 when I worked at a store. The store was empty and in came a Hindu woman. She looked like a princess and well could have been one. She bought some hanging costume jewelry from me. I was at the point of fainting. She had copper skin, long red hair, and the rest of her was perfect. A timeless beauty. When I had to charge her, I felt embarrassed. As if saying she understood and not to worry, she smiled at me. Then she disappeared and I have never again seen anyone like her. Sometimes I get the impression that she was the goddess Kali, the patron saint of thieves and goldsmiths, except Kali was also the goddess of murderers, and this Hindu woman was not only the most beautiful woman on earth, but she seemed also to be a good person—very sweet and considerate.

MM: Do you like dogs or cats?

RB: Female dogs, but I don't have any more pets.

MM: What do you remember of your childhood?

RB: Everything. I don't have one bad memory.

MM: Did you collect figurines?

RB: Yes, of soccer players and Hollywood actors and actresses.

MM: Did you have a scooter?

RB: My parents made the mistake of giving me a pair of roller skates when we lived in Valparaiso, a city made up of hills. The result was disastrous. Every time I put the skates on it was as if I was trying to commit suicide.

MM: What is your favorite soccer team?

RB: None right now. The ones who fall to second tier, then third consecutively, then regional until they've disappeared. The phantom teams.

MM: Which historical character would you have liked to resemble?

RB: Sherlock Holmes. Captain Nemo. Julien Sorel, our father. Prince Mishkin, our uncle. Alicia, our professor. And Houdini, who is a mix between Alicia, Sorel and Mishkin.

MM: Did you fall in love with older neighbors when you were young?

RB: Of course.

MM: Did the girls in your school pay any attention to you?

RB: I don't think so. At least I was convinced they did not.

MM: What do you owe the women in your life?

RB: Ever so much. A sense of defiance and high risk. For the sake of decency, I'll keep quiet about the other things.

MM: Do they owe you anything?

RB: Nothing.

MM: Have you suffered much for love?

RB: Very much the first time, then I learned to take things with a bit more humor.

MM: And what about hate?

A Mexican poet, Amado Nervo (1870–1919) was among the vanguard of nineteenth century Mexican poetry.

RB: Even if I sound somewhat pretentious, I've never hated anyone. At least I'm certain I am incapable of sustained hatred. And if the hatred is not sustained, it's not hatred, is it?

MM: How did you win the affection of your wife?

RB: Cooking rice for her. I was very poor at that time and my diet basically consisted of rice, so I learned to cook it in many different ways.

MM: Describe the day you became a father for the first time.

RB: It was night, a little before midnight. I was alone, and because you couldn't smoke in the hospital, I smoked a cigarette virtually perched on the cornice of the fourth floor. No one saw me from the street, only the moon, as **Amado Nervo** would have said. When I came back in, a nurse told me my son had just been born. He was very big, almost all bald, with open eyes as if asking himself who the devil had him in his arms.

MM: Will Lautaro be a writer?

RB: I hope only that he's happy. Thus, it would be better if he were something else. Airplane pilot, for example, plastic surgeon or editor.

MM: What do you recognize in him as your own?

RB: Luckily he resembles his mother much more than me.

MM: Do you worry about the position of your books on bestseller lists?

RB: Minimally.

MM: Do you think about your readers?

RB: Almost never.

MM: Of all the things your readers have said about your books, what has moved you the most?

RB: Quite simply, the readers themselves move me—the ones who dare to read Voltaire's *Philosophical Dictionary*, which is one of the most pleasant and modern works I know. I'm moved by the steely youth who read Cortázar and Parra, just as I read them and intend to continue reading them. I'm moved by those youths who sleep with a book under their head. A book is the best pillow that exists.

MM: What things have made you angry?

A Spanish poet, Leopoldo María Panero (b. 1948) was infamous for his wild lifestyle. Five of his poems were published in English translation in the Spring 2009 issue of *eXchanges*.

Jesús Ferrero (b. 1952) is a Spanish novelist, poet, and playwright. His major works include *Bélver Yin* (1981) and *Las noches rojas* (2003).

Darío Oses (b. 1949) is an important Chilean literary critic, specializing in the literature of the 1990s.

RB: At this age, getting angry is a waste of time. And, regrettably, time matters at my age.

MM: Have you ever feared your fans?

RB: I've feared **Leopoldo María Panero's** fans. On the one hand, he seems to me one of the three best living poets in Spain. During a cycle of readings organized by **Jesús Ferrero** in Pamplona, Panero closed the cycle and as the day of his reading neared, the neighborhood where our hotel was began to fill with freaks who looked like they had recently escaped an insane asylum. But on the other hand, they were the best readership any poet can aspire to reach. The problem was that some didn't just look crazy but like murderers too. Ferrero and I were afraid that at any moment someone might get up and say they had killed Leopoldo María Panero, then fired four shots at the head of the poet; and while they were at it, one at Ferrero and the last one at me.

MM: How does it feel to be regarded as the Latin American writer with the most promising future by critics like **Darío Osses**?

RB: It must be a joke. I am the Latin American writer with the least promising future. But on that point, I am the type with the most past, which is what matters anyway.

MM: Does the critical book being prepared by your compatriot **Patricia Espinosa** arouse your curiosity?

RB: Not at all. Apart from how I'll end up in her book, which I don't suppose will be very good, Espinosa seems to be a very good critic. But her work is necessary in Chile. In fact, the need for new critics—let's call her that—is urgent all over Latin America.

MM: And what about the Argentine **Celina Mazoni's** book?

RB: I know Celina personally and I'm very fond of her. I dedicated one of the stories from *Putas Asesinas* to her.

MM: What bores you?

RB: Empty discourse from the left. I take for granted the empty discourse from the right.

MM: What entertains you?

RB: To see my daughter Alexandra play. To eat breakfast at a bar by the sea and to eat a croissant while reading the paper. Borges' literature. Bioy's literature. **Bustos Domecq's** literature. Making love.

A professor of literary criticism at the University of Chile, Patricia Espinosa wrote a critical essay on Bolaño in 2003 entitled "Bolaño, un poeta junto al acantilado" (Bolaño, A Poet Close to the Cliff).

An Argentine writer, Celina Manzoni is a co-author of *Roberto Bolaño: La escritura como tauromaquia* (Roberto Bolaño: Writing as Bullfighting).

H. Bustos Domecq was a pseudonym used by Borges and Bioy Casares for collaborations.

MM: Do you write by hand?

RB: Poetry, yes. For the rest, I use an old computer from 1993.

MM: Close your eyes. Out of all the landscapes you've come across in Latin America, what comes to mind first?

RB: Lisa's lips in 1974. My father's broken-down bus on a desert road. The tuberculosis wing of a hospital in Cauquenes and my mother telling my sister and I to hold our breath. An excursion to Popocatépetl with Lisa, Mara, Vera and someone else I don't remember. But I do remember Lisa's lips, her extraordinary smile.

MM: What is heaven like?

RB: Like Venice, I'd hope, a place full of Italian men and women. A place you can use and wear down, a place that knows nothing will endure, including paradise, and knows that in the end at last it doesn't matter.

MM: And hell?

RB: It's like Ciudad Juárez, our curse and mirror, a disturbing reflection of our frustrations, and our infamous interpretation of liberty and of our desires.

MM: When did you know you were gravely ill?

RB: In 1992.

MM: What change did your illness have on your character?

RB: None. I knew I wasn't immortal, which at thirty-eight it was high time I learn.

MM: What do you wish to do before dying?

RB: Nothing special. Well, clearly I'd prefer not to die. But sooner or later the distinguished lady arrives. The problem is that sometimes she's neither a lady nor very distinguished, but, as Nicanor Parra says in a poem, she's a hot wench who will make your teeth chatter no matter how fancy you think you are.

MM: Whom would you like to encounter in the hereafter?

RB: I don't believe in the hereafter. Were it to exist, I'd be surprised. I'd enroll immediately in some course Pascal would be teaching.

MM: Have you ever thought about committing suicide?

RB: Of course. On one occasion I survived precisely because I knew how to kill myself if things got any worse.

MM: Have you ever believed you were going crazy?

RB: Of course, but I was always saved by my sense of humor. I'd tell myself stories that made me crazy with laughter. Or I'd remember situations that made me roll on the ground laughing.

MM: Madness, death and love. Which of these three things have you had more of in your life?

RB: I hope with all of my heart that it was love.

MM: What makes your jaw hurt laughing?

RB: The misfortunes of myself and others.

MM: What things make you cry?

RB: The same: the misfortunes of myself and others.

MM: Do you like music?

RB: Very much.

MM: Do you see your work the way your critics and readers see it: *The Savage Detectives* above all, then all the rest?

RB: The only novel that doesn't embarrass me is *Amberes*, maybe because it continues to be unintelligible. The bad reviews it has received are badges of honor from actual combat, not skirmishes with simulated fire. The rest of my "work" is not bad. They're entertaining novels. Time will tell if they're anything more. For now, they earn money, get translated and help me make very generous and kind friends. I can live, and live well, off literature, so complaining would be gratuitous and unfounded. The truth is I concede very little importance to my books. I am much more interested in the books of others.

MM: Would you not cut a few pages out of *The Savage Detectives*?

RB: No. In order to cut pages, I would have to reread it and my religion prohibits me that.

MM: Does it scare you that someone might want to make a film version of the novel?

RB: Oh, Mónica, I fear other things—much more terrifying things, infinitely more terrifying.

A French surrealist writer, Jacques Vaché (1895-1919) worked closely with André Breton in the foundation of surrealism. A collection of his works, *Jacques Vaché and the Roots of Surrealism*, is available in English.

Georg Christoph Lichtenberg (1742-1799) was a German scientist and satirist. A collection of his aphorisms is available in English as *The Waste Books*, 2000.

MM: Is "Silva the Eye" a tribute to Julio Cortázar?

RB: In no way.

MM: When you finished writing "Silva the Eye," didn't you feel you had probably written a story on the level of, say, "A House Taken Over"?

RB: When I finished writing "Silva the Eye" I stopped crying or something like it. What more could I want than for it to resemble a Cortázar story? Although "A House Taken Over" is not one of my favorites.

MM: Which five books have marked your life?

RB: In reality the five books are more like 5,000. I'll mention these only as the tip of the spear: *Don Quixote* by Cervantes, *Moby-Dick* by Melville. The complete works of Borges, *Hopscotch* by Cortázar, *A Confederacy of Dunces* by Toole. I should also cite *Nadja* by Breton, the letters of **Jacques Vaché**. *Anything Ubu* by Jarry, *Life: A User's Manual* by Perec. *The Castle* and *The Trial* by Kafka. *Aphorisms* by **Lichtenberg**. *The Tractatus* by Wittgenstein. *The Invention of Morel* by Bioy Casares. *The Satyricon* by Petronius. *The History of Rome* by Tito Livio. *Pensées* by Pascal.

MM: Do you get on well with your editor?

RB: Very well. Herralde is a very intelligent person and very often quite charming. Perhaps for me it would be more convenient if he weren't so charming. The truth is I've known him for eight years now and, at least for my part, the affection does nothing if not grow, as one bolero puts it. Even though it might perhaps be better for me if I didn't care for him so.

MM: What do you say to those who believe *The Savage Detectives* is the great contemporary Mexican novel?

RB: That they say it out of pity. They see that I'm down or fainting in public plazas and they can think of nothing better to say than a merciful lie, which, by the way, is the most appropriate thing in these cases, and it's not even a venial sin.

MM: Is it true that it was Juan Villoro who convinced you not to name your novel *By Night In Chile* "Shit Storms"?

RB: It was between Villoro and Herralde.

MM: From whom else do you take advice about your work?

Mexican poet, novelist, playwright, and essayist Carmen Boullosa (b. 1954) was highly regarded by Bolaño. An essay he wrote about her, entitled "Biena y la sombra de una mujer," appears in *Entre parentesis*, forthcoming in English from New Directions. She is also the co-host of a respected Spanish language television program, *Nueva York*.

Writer and editor Álvaro Enrique (b. 1969) is a postmodernist Mexican writer. None of his major works have been translated into English, but a short story, "On the Author's Death" is collected in the *Best of Contemporary Mexican Fiction*.

Mexican fiction writer, editor, and essayist Mauricio Montiel Figueroa (b. 1968) is one of the most lauded Mexican writers under forty. He has written several collections of short stories and a number of critical essays for various periodicals. See *Points of Departure: New Stories from Mexico*, 2001.

Along with Jorge Volpi and others, Mexican novelist and short story writer Ignacio Padilla (b. 1968) was a member of the "Crack Generation" that attempted to break the production of magical realism. *Shadow Without a Name* (2003), *Antipodes* (2004).

Mexican novelist and short story writer Sergio Pitol (b. 1933) was awarded the Cervantes Prize in 2005 for his work *El mago de Viena* (2005).

RB: I don't listen to advice from anybody, not even my doctor. I wildly dole out advice, but I don't heed any.

MM: How is Blanes?

RB: It's a nice little town. Or a very small city of 30,000 inhabitants. Quite nice. It was founded 2,000 years ago by the Romans, then people from all over started passing through. It's not a rich person's resort but a proletariat's. Workers from the north and the east. Some stay to live forever. The bay is most beautiful.

MM: Do you miss anything about your life in Mexico?

RB: My youth, and endless walks with Mario Santiago.

MM: Which Mexican writer do you admire profoundly?

RB: Many. From my generation I admire Sada, whose writing project I find the most bold, Villoro and **Carmen Boullosa**. Among the young writers, I am very interested in what **Álvaro Enrique** and **Mauricio Montiel** are doing, as well as Volpi and **Ignacio Padilla**. I continue to read **Sergio Pitol**, who

ROBERTO BOLAÑO (1950–2003) was a Chilean poet, novelist, and essayist. His translated work includes *Amulet, By Night in Chile, Distant Star, Nazi Literature in the Americas, The Savage Detectives, 2666, Last Evenings on Earth, The Romantic Dogs,* and *The Skating Rink.* His last years were spent in Blanes, on Spain's Mediterranean coast.

Interviewers **HÉCTOR SOTO** and **MATÍAS BRAVO** interviewed Bolaño for the Chilean magazine *Capital.* Both were writers for the magazine; Soto was also a co-owner.

Interviewer **CARMEN BOULLOSA**'s 2002 interview with Bolaño appeared in *Bomb*, a Brooklyn-based arts and culture magazine. Boullosa is a highly regarded Mexican novelist, poet, essayist, and television personality. She is the co-host of the respected Spanish-language television program *Nueva York.* An essay Bolaño wrote about Boullosa, entitled "Biena y la sombra de una mujer," appears in *Entre parentesis*, forthcoming in English from New Directions.

ELISEO ÁLVAREZ interviewed Bolaño shortly before his death. The interview was published posthumously in 2005 by the Barcelona literary journal *Turia.*

The final interview given by Bolaño appeared in the Mexican edition of *Playboy* magazine in July 2003. It was conducted via e-mail by **MÓNICA MARISTAIN** who, at the time, was the magazine's editor-in-chief. Maristain is an Argentine editor, journalist, and writer. In 1992 she was named journalist of the year in Argentina for her coverage of the Barcelona Olympics. She has written for various national and international media outlets and published two books of poetry, *Transfusiones al óleo* and *Drinking Thelonious*. She lives in Mexico.

MARCELA VALDES is a contributing editor at *Publishers Weekly* and the books editor for *The Washington Examiner*. In 2000, she co-founded *Críticas*, a U.S. magazine devoted to the coverage of Spanish-language books, and in 2009 she was awarded a Nieman Fellowship in Arts & Culture Journalism at Harvard University. Her writing appears regularly *in The Washington Post* and *The Nation*, among other publications.

Translator **SYBIL PEREZ**, a native of Chicago, is an editor at *Stop Smiling* magazine, a post she has held for over ten years.